LIVING WISDOM

LIVING WISDOM

Growing in the Life of Prayer

Nicholas Turner

First published in Great Britain 1995
Society for Promoting Christian Knowledge
Holy Trinity Church
Marylebone Road
London NW1 4DU

British Library Cataloguing-in-Publication Data
A catalogue record for this book is available
from the British Library

ISBN 0-281-04857-6

Typeset by Pioneer Associates, Perthshire
Printed in Great Britain by
The Cromwell Press, Melksham, Wiltshire

Contents

Acknowledgements

These chapters first emerged as a series of seminars for students at St Stephen's House, Oxford, twelve years ago. The seed had been sown a decade before that from a short, austere essay by Simone Weil, entitled *Reflections on the Right Use of School Studies with a View to the Love of God*, written in 1942 for her mentor Father Perrin, and included in the collection *Waiting for God*. Most of the ideas then grew and developed within parish groups and on retreats, and I am grateful to all those who shared their wisdom and insight.

The actual writing I have done here on Ascension, a barren rock in the middle of the ocean. It has its advantages. With a population of only a thousand, there is the time; so far from the rest of the world, there is little distraction; without a library, there is no temptation to consult yet another authority. I must simply take pen and paper, and sit and write. Which is not to say that my mind does not wander. I can look up and see the heavy, regular waves crashing into the bay, relics of a storm five thousand miles away. Those waves, that vast ocean and the rock against which it strikes have influenced my thoughts, though how I do not know.

I would like to thank in particular Bishop Geoffrey Rowell of Basingstoke for his encouragement, RAF Ascension for their support, and above all my wife, the Revd Ann Turner, for much typing and continuing wise advice.

These pages have taken many years to mature and I hope

they are the better for it. Further growth and refinement might have been distracting. If wisdom is a pearl of great price, then this little book is not the oyster – it is the oyster knife. Useful, even perhaps valuable, but in the end only a tool, and not to be confused with the goal itself.

Happy is the man that findeth wisdom,
And the man that getteth understanding.
For the merchandise of it is better
   than the merchandise of silver,
and the gain thereof than fine gold.
She is more precious than rubies:
and all the things thou canst desire
   are not to be compared unto her.
Length of days is in her right hand;
and in her left hand riches and honour.
Her ways are ways of pleasantness,
and all her paths are peace.

Proverbs 3.13–17 (AV)

Introduction

A Path to Wisdom

Wisdom is a grace, and so cannot be earned. There will always be others who appear to have received more than a fair share through no merit of their own. Is it then worth setting out to gain wisdom, when it cannot be grasped nor guaranteed?

To pierce the mystery, to understand a hidden depth of creation, to touch some part of the truth: these are some of the gifts of wisdom. It will not pay the rent, nor heal a broken love affair, nor even advance a life's ambition. Yet it remains a great gift. Its value cannot be counted, but only felt, as for example in the sense of awe at God's compassion, in the thanks of a friend for a way out of the maze, or in the opening of a vision for a beleaguered community.

It is a gift because it is God's wisdom, which he shares with those who wait upon him. As such it is its own reward and justification; nevertheless, God does allow us just enough compensation in the improvement of life, the solving of problems and the appreciation of others, to encourage a quiet pursuit of yet more of this gift.

True wisdom is not competitive, does not foster envy and yet urges us to seek more. It becomes not so much an achievement of thought as a process or journey that leads to a deeper understanding of the human heart and the ways of God and humankind.

Study can be a path to wisdom. Not only through the subject matter that is studied, but also by the act of studying itself. It is this act of studying, and not its content, which is explored in these pages.

Study, whether the academic discipline of college, or the demands of a job, or the product of our leisure, can do this because it can teach us prayer, and indeed become prayer. By prayer I mean not asking God for things, but listening to him, discerning his purpose, opening our hearts to his grace – walking with him, hearing and receiving his holy word, heeding his children and the needs of the world.

Part One

Come back,
keep peace,
and you will be saved . . .
Isaiah 30.15

Chapter 1

Learning How to Listen

Is it ever easy to listen to God? It depends on what you mean. In a fast-paced and confusing world, full of passing ideas and conflicting claims, the call of God in the Ten Commandments or in the words of Jesus, may appear by contrast to be crystal clear. Yet at another level, hearing the voice of God, not for the world in general for every generation, but for oneself in particular, now, can seem unfathomably difficult, if not impossible to comprehend.

Are you a good listener? This is an unfair question, because you know that you ought to be, and you know that you ought to be better, which makes it hard to reply either 'Yes' or 'No'. It makes better sense to put it more impersonally: What makes a good listener? It is not simply a matter of warmth, tact and a pleasing personality. Nor can it be goodwill, the best intentions and an interest in other people. It is not that these qualities are not valuable, even vital; but they speak only of the conditions within which the true quality of listening can be used effectively.

Listening is a grace. Whether listening to God or to our neighbour, the ability is itself a free gift from God. This is important to understand, for the one thing that is most certain is that this ability does not come as the result of strenuous, determined, tiring effort; it is never the guaranteed product or reward for hard work. Grace cannot be earned, but (and this is a common truth of the Christian life) we can learn to place ourselves in a position to receive it. This is an essentially negative process, the exclusion of distractions, the exclusion of self, the focusing on 'the one thing necessary'.

Let me put it this way. A person of goodwill, and not necessarily a Christian, has a strong desire to be a good listener to his or her neighbour. One might these days call it counselling, or just 'helping people' in sorrow or difficulty. It is a widespread desire, to be able to offer more than just sympathy to someone who unburdens herself of some deep and painful problem; to help that person, and many others. Beyond a comfortable chair, quiet surroundings and a cup of coffee, what can you offer to your friend in need? How can you hear what she is really saying between the tears, the anger, the silences, the confusion and embarrassment? How do *you* understand what she is trying to say?

Probably the most common answer is 'experience', having been through the same thing yourself. 'I know what you are going through'. Experience teaches, it is claimed. Does it? Suppose for the moment that it does. You are young and full of idealism and want to enter one of the caring professions, you want to help people with their problems and to be a good listener. How are you going to do it? By accumulating as many experiences as you can? Bereavement, unemployment, divorce, disease. Even if you could acquire suffering, or travel through it like a tourist, would it teach you? Does not experience (excuse the irony) show us that it can just as easily make people embittered, withdrawn, angry, twisted or selfish?

The Christian tradition has always insisted that we can learn from experience, but never that experience teaches. It is important to insist on the point, because it can indeed be a great source of comfort, when you are troubled, to find someone else who has been through the same experience, who knows what you are feeling; you would more willingly pour out your grief to such a person, because they understand. But it is not quite the same if you are the listener; you cannot offer your own experience or suffering. To pour in a double measure of troubles is not good listening; 'I know what you are going through' can be a way of avoiding the need to take in what someone is saying, or even of distracting attention from their pain to yours. At times it can sound deeply wounding and uncaring.

If experience can make you bitter, it can also, even more easily, make you blasé. When someone comes to you, half your age, don't their problems sometimes seem very boring? Unrequited teenage love for example. When you have been told the same thing for the fourth or fifth time, it is in part your own experience that makes it sound so dull. For you really do know what he is talking about. You could almost write the script. I confess, with shame, that this has happened to me many times: experience does not make listening easier. If you have been through the same thing yourself then you may already know the answer, the solution to the pain. In giving it, you have most probably ceased to listen.

I can give a precise example, which has haunted me ever since. I was a newly ordained curate, in a terraced house in Manchester, still rather lost and lonely in this new and alien world. It was a Thursday evening, I had said Evening Prayer and was collecting together some walking things for an early start for the Peak District on my Friday day off. I'd make some supper and go soon to bed. Then there was a knock at the door. A young woman of about my age and rather attractive, 'Could I have a talk?' But of course. Like other young clergy, what I wanted to do most was to help people, people with problems, and here was such a person, with the added merit of being young and pretty as well.

It gradually became clear that there wasn't going to be any possibility of a romantic friendship and that her problem wasn't very interesting; in fact, as time drew on, and I grew tired and impatient, it became quite commonplace and boring. I knew the answer (for I had learned from experience), so in the end I gave it. And that was the end of that. Did she ever return? No, of course not, I had given the answer, and I had stopped listening. Sloth, that's what it was, laziness, one of the seven deadly sins. Walking over the hills the next day, I had time to rehearse the excuses and the shame, and to learn that listening is not easy.

Let us suppose, to take a standard, hypothetical example popularly used against the Church, that you are a celibate, male priest, whose counsel is being sought by a married woman in the throes of a painful divorce. Being neither married, nor a woman, you would manifestly have nothing to fall back on, no experience to draw upon. What do you have to offer? Only the most concentrated and undivided attention will catch the crucial whisper and perceive the truth. And how is that attention possible? Perhaps in part because you have no experience of your own to distract you.

That still does not provide an answer, but it is not necessarily an answer as such that is needed, at least not an answer from you. Those who speak of a wise and saintly confessor often refer to some gentle, seemingly trivial, question that somehow broke the guilt and fear and opened the heart to the love and forgiveness of God. Not a solution, but a question, a phrase or a word. How does that word come?

How is it that from the darkness the word suddenly emerges, as if by its own creation? It is a grace of the Holy Spirit – and yet it will only emerge after a deep and seemingly formless concentration. How? How do we connect through this darkness? It is something we have to learn.

I do not remember now which section of the Theology course I had expected to find the most rewarding, but I do remember the surprise at discovering, looking back upon completion, that it had been New Testament Greek – that daunting discipline whose mastery had so dominated the first year of study and which I would readily have avoided had it been possible.

It was not because I could now read the Gospels and the other sacred writings in the original, exciting and valuable as that is. It was not the Greek itself, the goal, but the learning of that Greek, the journey, which proved to be the clearest and most effective spiritual discipline of the whole course.

The learning of a 'dead' language offers no short cuts. When speaking a modern language, on holiday for example, tone of voice, facial expressions and sign language are all part of the process, and can on occasions work wonders; the task here is communication, of which the language itself is only part, albeit a very large one. Nor does a dead language offer room for bluffing, waffling, padding out and side-tracking, which prove such beguiling temptations when writing an essay in, say, History or Sociology. There is no place for wit, flair or originality – almost, it might seem, no place for intelligence.

There is an attractive counter-balancing justice in this: the more difficult and unappealing a subject appears, the more valuable it can be as a means to learning how to listen. The fewer marks you can realistically hope for from an earthly teacher, the more you can learn from your heavenly teacher about prayer. Simone Weil gives the striking example of St Jean Vianney, the Curé d'Ars, patron saint of parish clergy and one of history's greatest confessors. As a seminary student, he had immense difficulty learning Latin, so much so that his ordination was postponed more than once on account of his failure to make the grade. Those years of studious struggle never bore fruit in his mastery of the language, but rather in his awesome ability to listen, that drew so many thousands to his confessional. If Jean Vianney had on the contrary been good at languages, perhaps he would not have been a saint.

How then is this capacity to listen achieved? One of the simplest, and most oft-repeated, exercises in the learning of a language is the revision of vocabulary. Let us suppose that you have written a list of words to be learned in a notebook, the English words on the left-hand side of the page, the Greek, or whichever, on the right. Finding a few moments free, you decide to revise. You open the book and cover the words on the right-hand side with a piece of card. You look at the first word in the left-hand column; if you immediately remember the Greek equivalent, that is fine, and you can move on to the next word. But if you do not, then what? In that single moment, repeated endlessly, *before* you pull the card down a quarter of an inch to reveal the answer, there is listening.

It is so clear and so simple a lesson, it is worth pausing awhile and reflecting on it. If you still have such a vocabulary notebook, look it out; if not, try to remember your last one and how you used it. When that foreign word would not come, what did you do in that moment, before you gave up and lifted the card? What can you do? You know that you have come across the word before, since you wrote it down yourself; yet now you have not the faintest idea. There are no clues to be sought and no short cut is offered. You can only listen, to the impenetrable silence, and wait, for the word to come. You do not always succeed, but that does not matter too much; for the moment it is not the language we are after, but the training for listening. Before analysing this further, we can consider other more complex examples.

Take next a full sentence from the Greek New Testament itself, or from any other ancient text. We have here not simply an individual word, but a whole complex construction, which poses a number of problems, problems created by the gaps in one's knowledge. How does one effectively deal with these blanks and with what appears to be only partial information? To the Greek scholar it may all seem very straightforward: to the poor student it can be an immensely confusing, seemingly impossible task. One word is bad enough but several all interrelated is many times worse. All one can offer is patient, painstaking attention to every detail; and how desperately difficult that is.

Consider finally a complete page or paragraph of text, such as an account of Jesus's ministry or a passage of Paul's teaching to the Early Church. The sheer panic at the enormity of the task, the overwhelming fear of never being able to make any progress towards its translation. So much work, so little knowledge to work with. If it were easy and enjoyable, we would know what to do, and do it; that it is neither in fact changes nothing: you simply need greater attention, and the patience to apply it.

These are the moments when the art of prayer and the grace of listening are presented to us with startling clarity, when you yourself are centre stage and your mind is on the line and put to the test. There is nothing else that you can do (at present), no reading, no preparation, no listening to a teacher; just your mind, alone, listening to this foreign language, waiting for the answer, waiting for the truth.

Melodramatic? Perhaps. Yet surely there is a real gain in dramatizing the situation, in developing a vivid sense of the difficulties involved. To translate a passage of the Greek New Testament, which has already been translated, and translated better, by hundreds of scholars throughout the Christian centuries, is not obviously a worthwhile achievement, especially when it proves so hard to attain. But to put your own person and character to the test, in a patient waiting upon the truth, to stand at the edge of darkness and perceive the emergence of an elusive revelation, that *is* a challenge.

How do you listen to a Greek sentence? The important point to remember is that it is an essentially negative task. If you find your muscles tensing, your brow furrowing or your fist tightening, whether literally or metaphorically, then you have got it wrong.

The image we need is not of climbing a mountain, a visible and attainable goal, however distant, towards which we may have to struggle wearily, doggedly putting one foot in front of the other to the point of sheer effort and willpower. The correct image can be found on the same mountain, but demanding altogether different skills. You have come to see some elusive wildlife, a woodchuck, a pine marten, or a golden eagle: the task here is to find the right spot and sit and wait, without movement or sound, with enormous patience and your eyes open, waiting for the shy animal to show.

If the stress is on relaxation rather than effort, it follows that a few moments of deliberate relaxation and a loosening

of any tense muscles before you begin to study will be helpful. This exhortation is now a commonplace in any book on
prayer, accompanied sometimes with precise breathing exercises; the fact that it is so widely urged as to seem obvious
makes it no less valuable, especially if you fully understand
why.

An absence of distraction is also vital, but that does not
make it any easier. It is not merely that there are other tasks
more attractive than study itself, but that even within the
subject of study it is more pleasurable and less demanding to
read a book or listen to a lecture than to do the hard work
yourself. Worst of all, and this can be quite upsetting if you
are not prepared for it, is the fact that once you have put
aside the temptations and emptied your mind to listen, that
is precisely the opportunity a whole array of thoughts have
been waiting for – that telephone call you should have
made, that vital item for the shopping list, that overdue
book to return to the library . . . . It is as though these
thoughts had been waiting around the corner for the
moment your mind was free, so that what was supposed to
be a quiet moment of prayer or study becomes instead a cold
sweat of panic at all the things you had forgotten.

It may seem very unfair, but it could hardly be otherwise
if you think about it. If your life is full and busy, with all the
competing demands of your job, your health, your family,
your friends, and the world around you, then your mind is
full. You do not have to be thinking for your mind to be
filled; watching a film, looking out of the window, reading a
book, can all provide you with enough impressions, memories and emotions to fill your consciousness. Cut out all this
material and deliberately empty your mind, and you create
precisely the opportunity needed for everything you had
forgotten or were trying to avoid.

There is not a great deal you can do about it, and certainly no point in fighting against it. It is rather like the old
trick, 'Think about anything you like, but don't think about
hippopotamuses'. You cannot stop the thoughts coming; all
you can do is let them affect you as little as possible, just let

them wash over you. It is the same with insomnia, as you are tossed about with fears and worries and plans, distracting your mind from sleep. Perhaps a time for prayer during the day would be a cure for insomnia at night – but that is getting off the subject.

Distractions are a particular problem when studying, for they not only remind you of themselves, but so easily change to temptations. They offer (so it seems) simple and achievable tasks, so much more worthwhile than the hard work of concentration, which by contrast can appear so formless and with no guaranteed achievement, in short impossible. In such moments it is most important to remember that learning a foreign language is more like car maintenance than philosophy.

To the question, 'What is the meaning of life?' there may be no answer; indeed it may even be the wrong question to ask. 'What has gone wrong with this car?', however, has a precise and practical solution, achievable sometimes even with the wrong questions. There *is* a solution: even when you do not hear the answer, you have the assurance that it is there to be discovered. This is another reason why foreign languages are, and always have been, a particularly effective means of learning how to listen.

You have the problem in front of you, a Greek sentence. You can be certain there is a solution, a complete and coherent English sentence. You must listen to the first in order to arrive at the second. Listening is patience. As you build up the English sentence in your mind, from simple words you immediately recognize, then by analysing the word endings, the conjugations and declensions, to the verb, subject, object and so on, you are seeking to bring together all the information before you into *the* complete and coherent whole. If you are a skilled linguist you might toy with the nuances and play with different paraphrases to mirror the precise emphasis you detect in the original. If you are a poor linguist and struggling, your mind will seize on any hypothesis which suggests that it can fulfil the task of being an accurate translation.

Here is the greatest danger. The simple, and perhaps
natural desire to get out of the problem can blind you to a
whole host of inconsistencies in your particular solution.
Now that you have grasped *an* answer, there is a strong
temptation to ignore them, to suggest that they are not
there. I can still remember a Latin class at school, when the
master clipped me round the ears (it was nearly 30 years
ago) for a 'stupid' translation. 'But I thought . . . ' I said, as I
pointed to the two words I believed I knew. 'But you *didn't*
think,' he replied. I hated him for being right.

When you mistranslate a sentence, the chances are very
high that impatience was at least part of the cause. Maybe
you did not know every word or construction, and with your
partial knowledge could not have been expected to give a
perfect answer, but by your impatience you still did not
bring out all that you did know. What you failed to do
was to go on paying careful attention, to continue waiting
patiently, for more of the meaning to emerge off the page.

Such waiting, though selfless, empty, formless, even
relaxed, is the height of concentration; it is not, however
simple it may appear to be in theory, learned quickly, and it
cannot be sustained for long periods without considerable
practice. It is important to emphasize this, for when one is
shown the right answer by a teacher or the New Testament
itself, one's stupidity can seem overwhelming. An answer to
the meaning of life can still be debated; a mechanical solution or a translation can seem so obvious once given that it
is vital not to forget that its achievement is not necessarily,
because of that, easy.

Consider an entirely non-academic pursuit. Target shooting is a superb discipline of prayer. I hesitate to say this as a
priest; somehow handling rifles isn't quite the thing, and I
have not done so for many years, but I thoroughly enjoyed
it when I did. Once you have adjusted the rifle, especially
the sights, to yourself, and yourself to whatever you are lying
on, all you have to do is point the rifle at the centre of the
target, press the trigger and hit the bull. It is a task so simple
it is banal. So why do you not gain a perfect score every

time? One's failure is fascinating. How can it be so difficult to do something so simple? That's what makes it so enjoyable as a sport.

Consider painting. It has the disadvantage over a foreign language in not having a clear, assured answer, but most people would find it a lot more enjoyable. Forget for the moment the problems of draughtsmanship and even the problems of colours and how to mix them, and concentrate on the tones. Once again, the task stated on paper is remarkably simple. You have whatever it is in front of you, a collection of objects on a table; you can see them clearly, they are familiar to you. There is nothing intellectual here, this is seeing, distinguishing the light and the dark. How extraordinary then that it should be so difficult and demand so much care and patient attention.

'But *how* do I pay attention?' you scream to yourself after a few months of learning Greek, shooting or painting. 'It's not coming!' you want to moan, as no progress seems evident. 'But that is the whole point,' one is forced to reply. Listening, paying attention to God is not a simple technique that you can expect to acquire step by step; it is not painting by numbers. Its essentially negative character, the lack of strenuous intellectual effort, the lack of ideas, imagination and invention, the lack of any obvious involvement of one's self, of one's own experience, make it hard to delineate, and hard to determine progress.

You cannot see it coming, but one day it will have arrived. You cannot judge your progress by what you *feel* now, but by comparing how it was six months or a year ago. And it *will* come. Easy to say, rather more difficult to believe.

Chapter 2

Acquiring Self-knowledge

'Let us confess our sins.' This is the most frequent call to the congregation at the beginning of all types of Christian worship. To help us celebrate the mystery of the Eucharist, we first recall our need for the sacrament; that we may worthily praise the Lord, we first seek to be cleansed from our sins; to know God's unconditional love, we first acknowledge what has separated us from that love. There are a hundred different contexts and descriptions of why we do it; for it is a natural first step in both private prayer and public worship.

It is the grace of God that matters most, his love for us, not our imperfect love for him, so that we must be aware that too much stress on our own sins can lead to mere self-obsession. But it always has been a central theme of the Christian tradition that we must deliberately and conscientiously make ourselves aware of our precise need of God's grace. If we have no sin, we shall receive no grace: therefore we seek to know our sins, that we may know God's grace.

No sin, no grace. It has always surprised me that sin has had such a bad press within Christianity, and why it is so sharply differentiated from the grace of God. I can understand why this dark and utterly vile monster, lurking deep within us and an object of pure revulsion, makes such a fine rhetorical device for the hell-fire preacher, but why has this particular image of sin been so persuasive to a wider, saner Christian public? For in practice, in our ordinary lives, with all their ups and downs and haphazard progress (so far removed from the clear cut image of St George slaying the dragon), sin and grace are learned together. The realization that you are a sinner is itself a gift of grace.

The Old Testament is full of encouraging examples in this regard. The great reason for hope in the Prophets is in the ringing tones of their condemnation, for God only convicts us of sin in order to teach us, reform us, and lead us to a deeper understanding of his grace. The very word 'confession' in Hebrew prevents the separation of the two themes, for it is the same word *yadah* that is used to praise God for his grace and goodness as to admit and recount our human sinfulness. Knowledge of the one leads to a greater knowledge of the other, and so on, back and forth. This is seen in many of the psalms, most clearly Psalm 106, or in the great prayers of confession, my own favourite being Daniel 9.

The minister may begin, 'Let us call to mind our sins.' Let us quietly and deliberately bring them to mind, not simply offer for God's forgiveness whatever lies immediately to hand; let us search out and bring to the surface the evil we have done and the good we have failed to do, all that separates us from the love of God. *How* do we call to mind our sins? To suppose that good intentions are sufficient is to misunderstand the nature and gravity of sin. Most people have good intentions; but do most people naturally understand themselves to be sinners? I think not. It requires knowledge, a self-knowledge that has to be learned.

Some shameful deeds constantly return to trouble us. Far more misdeeds remain discreetly hidden, perhaps because we subconsciously suppress their memory, more probably because we remain insensitive to the harm we have done. Other more complex sins of silence, that we may share with a whole society, will take considerable maturity to discover and unearth. Even when we do manage to call them to mind, the task of self-knowledge does not end there; we may admit *that* we have sinned, but not so easily *how* we have sinned.

Self-knowledge requires self-examination, and that has to

be learned as a skill. Memory does not, by itself, offer to our gaze the dull, mediocre, inadequate parts of our lives. So how do we teach it to work harder on our behalf?

As with the art of listening, learning the skill of self-examination can be helped by considering the analogy with study. Take an essay, a report, a painting, whatever. It is your own work. Even if you have copied it from someone else, it was created by your own hand, and you are wholly responsible. It has clear, exact edges, a beginning and an end, and it is yours. The problem with memory is that it changes and cannot always be objectively corroborated, whereas a piece of work is simply there. Of course that piece of work isn't quite your 'self', it is rather more narrow and limited in scope. It is not a life, but that is also an advantage. Its limited scope makes it a better tool for learning the skill of self-examination.

You are a priest; it is Sunday evening, and you have preached your sermon. You are a student; the seminar has finished and your essay is handed back. You have delivered your talk to a meeting of the historical society, and returned home. A report you wrote for work has been duly circulated, and is now back on your desk. What is the next thing you should do? (I mean in relation to that subject: playing a game, walking the dog, or any other relaxation is something else entirely.) Back on the treadmill, as rector, student, worker or speaker, with one task completed, what do you do next? Our strong and natural desire is to put it away and get on with the next task, the *next* sermon, essay, talk or report. Wrong!

The thing you ought to do is to re-read that finished piece of work. Its life has come to an end: there is nothing that can usefully be corrected or improved. Now is the opportunity, by a slow, careful re-reading, to discover what went wrong and where it failed. The question is precise, '*What* did I do wrong?' and the answer is required not in general terms but in precise detail. A principle misunderstood, an idea taken from somewhere else and misplaced, a confused expression, a foolish non sequitur, a gap in the chain of reasoning, vague platitudes, total irrelevancies, all these are common faults in any subject.

It is unfortunate and frustrating but something we have all experienced, that mistakes and errors so often reveal themselves only when the work is completed and delivered. Even if no one says a word, you now know failings in a sermon, after you have preached it, that no amount of painstaking revision and practice could extract before. It is these failures that we now hope to pinpoint and examine by this careful re-reading.

Carried away by over-earnestness and wishing to be humble, wanting to make a full 'confession', we may be very keen to admit our failings, but that is not the same as truly knowing them. The aim is not to grovel, but to gain understanding; not self-abasement but self-knowledge. It is not an easy task, for you are seeking to understand your faults of intelligence, with no better instrument than your own intelligence, with all its faults.

Another advantage of analysing a piece of 'study' is that it shows how little help one can expect from others. People naturally prefer to praise and to offer encouragement; they may be induced to let slip that they think it wrong, foolish or incomprehensible, but as to detailed criticisms, that is highly unlikely. We are all prone to comment on other people's character rather than the product of their study. Even if such studied judgement were given, its help would be limited; the exercise is one of *self*-knowledge; though difficult, it is that which must be learned. Just as we confess our own sins, not other people's.

The clearest advantage, however, of this style of self-examination is that it is so mundane, even boring. When we speak of 'sin' in our lives, we tend to think of the exciting sins. You may be overwhelmed by guilt at an act of adultery, but you may also, and at the same time, be excited by the remembrance of it; in this context, calling to mind your sin may actually suppress the guilt and remorse in favour of the enjoyment of the reminder. The fear of being caught for doing wrong can add exhilaration to a sin, and to the memory of it.

No such excitement attaches to a sermon or an essay. Your sins here are dull, perhaps shaming, perhaps embarrassing, but hardly enjoyable to recall. That is why the task of re-reading is an unattractive one, and needs an effort of will to perform, and also why it is so useful, for in fact most of our sins are dull, not the result of exciting wickedness, but ordinary, repeated failure. That is how it is, and that is what we examine.

Having assembled a list that answers the question, 'What did I do wrong?', the next is, 'Why did I get it wrong?' This is an even harder question to answer.

First to be cleared away are the irrelevant answers, irrelevant that is in relation to yourself. If you were supplied with false information or bad advice, that is not going to tell you much about yourself. True, to be the victim of bad advice every time may be your problem not others', but we are not concerned with that here.

Why did you make the mistakes and errors that you did? Our first reaction is probably to say, 'I don't know.' I shall outline a number of possibilities. The most usual cause of error is very much the same as with listening. Simone Weil calls it impatience. I have always understood it as laziness. Perhaps one could call it 'snatching'. If pride is the deadliest sin in our ordinary lives, this lack of patience, of attention, of waiting, is the deadliest sin on the path of wisdom. In any piece of work, which is the object of this exercise in self-knowledge, look first for this failure to listen and wait for the truth to come, this snatching at some solution short of the truth itself.

Most obviously, since days are short, this could be a failure to spend sufficient time on the task you set yourself. You perhaps began an essay, a sermon, a painting, with great care and bursting with good intentions; each word or brush-stroke was made with solemn precision and attention. But as the argument or colour scheme develops and becomes more complicated, it begins to get out of control: more and more threads have to be linked, until in frustration you draw it all together with a single bold theme of thought or paint, a conclusion is reached and the frustration eased. As one who has listened to many a student essay, I can say without doubt this is the most common fault; however much time is spent on the beginning, the end is nearly always rushed.

Very often such impatience is deliberate, in the sense that you had a reason for it, good or bad and not necessarily related to the studying. Often, and more seriously, it is quite hidden from your consciousness, and so needs more careful examination. At the time of studying and writing, let us suppose, you hit on a brilliant theory that solves the problem you have been set; whether your own or someone else's, it seems to solve all your dilemmas, and you dash it off in high confidence. Looking back after the event, however, you find it superficial, inexact and full of holes. So ask yourself whether it was not, unconsciously, simply a way of cutting short all the stress and difficulty of considering so intractable a problem: your enthusiasm was not so much for its valid merits and seeming elegance, as for its (invalid) usefulness in answering your own problem of impatience.

'Why did I get it wrong?' A second possibility may be the influence of past patterns of thought. This appears a more obviously intellectual problem, less moral in character than impatience. A simple example of this is the geometric puzzle known as a tangram, in which you are given seven differently shaped blocks of wood that are to be fitted together to form a perfect square. The puzzle is made more difficult in those cases where you are first given three, then five, and only then all seven shapes, to create ever larger squares: the solutions you have learned in the first two cases make it even more difficult to solve the final one. The pattern which works for the first two stages is most definitely not the one that proves needful for the third. The use of your intelligence in the past is the basis for, but also a hindrance to, its use in the present.

There used to be a car-sticker and wall poster, once immensely popular, which cheerfully proclaimed, 'Today is the first day of the rest of your life.' While one may warm to its optimism, one should beware its ignorance of sin. We can be forgiven our sins, wholly and completely, but this does not mean the effect of that sin will instantly vanish. A repentant alcoholic can be forgiven in a moment, but the return to health will take longer. So too with study. In every piece of work we carry not only the effects of past failures and sloth, but also the patterns of thought learned years before. Yesterday was the first day of your life. We must therefore examine that yesterday and know its constraints.

It may seem unfair to call this yesterday a sin, but even if it was not, in itself, particularly sinful, it may provide the context for sin. If you had been brought up in a narrow, patriarchal society, you might be forgiven for being sexist in attitude on your arrival as a young man in a modern, cosmopolitan city. Forgiven perhaps, but not absolved of responsibility for actively broadening your moral understanding of women and men. You would be foolish and wrong to suppose you could supersede the ingrained attitudes of your background by a simple act of goodwill. In our moral lives we all rely more or less heavily on our upbringing, and that includes its faults.

Other reasons for error? There is a whole range of possibilities, some more obviously related to our character. Could your writing be motivated by bitterness over your unrecognized successes? Is your report for the chairman driven by envy of a colleague? Is your sermon fuelled by resentment of your congregation? Is your information constrained by avarice, an unwillingness to share with others the fruits of your investigation? No clear, accusing finger jumps off the page. It will be a subtle, elusive search, but you may eventually come face to face not only with the limitations of your intelligence but also of your personality, for they are inextricably interrelated.

It may be, even after patient self-examination, that you simply have no idea at all why you wrote what you did, or failed to see what is now so evident. When a child is asked, 'Why did you do that?' and replies, 'I don't know', it is often an attempt to avoid the full implications of the wrongdoing, to avoid the stare of the parent or teacher who stands there in infuriated patience, insisting, 'But you must know. Tell me *why* you did it.' Sometimes it truly is the full answer; sin is sometimes so stupid, we don't know why we did it. You re-read your essay, and you have not the slightest idea why you thought that.

Once again, we face the problem of inadequate intelligence analysing the faults of inadequate intelligence. Because we are sinners, even our confession of sin is flawed, which is why the dangers of an excessive and extravagant self-examination have (on the whole) been warned against and avoided in the Christian tradition. In the end there is much, this side of heaven, immune to our best analysis. But even if we cannot understand such errors, we can neither ignore them.

It is unlikely you would ever come up with a full range of 'sins' in any single reconsideration of your work. This is not a formal exercise, like a church confession, and not to be indulged in to excess. If I re-read every Sunday's sermon with such rigour, I think I would be more discouraged than enlightened, but from time to time, and usually with those I think to be my better, more successful ones, I do find the quiet and take the time, and it is a gentle lesson in self-knowledge.

Every Christian would assent to the notion of sin. Most would readily accept the idea of original sin. But the doctrine of total depravity? That seems to go just a bit too far; even the title seems offensive. The original doctrine, given expression by John Calvin, and developed by his followers, appears to suggest that fallen human nature is so depraved that each and every one of our faculties is useless to salvation, and what is more, that study and reason are a waste of time and inevitably ineffectual (in which case of course this book is also a waste of time). It is however a useful doctrine if its insistence reminds us that every part of human nature, without exception, is depraved and tainted by sin and the fall.

Sin, in other words, is to be found as much in what we do well as in what we do badly. This is an important lesson, and one not easy to learn. I became a committed Christian, as with so many teenagers of my generation, under the influence of a popular paperback *The Cross and the Switchblade*, which told of an evangelist's experiences in the roughest part of New York. The central character was a convert who had once been a gang leader, wielding a knife, dealing in drugs and unremittingly wicked: he had been saved and had truly and vividly passed from darkness to light. As quiet children in quiet England, we too longed to emulate so real and dramatic a conversion. We had, so it seemed, to dress up our petty sins, colour them, enlarge them, even exaggerate them, until we reached the level of wickedness worthy of a conversion to the gospel. How we longed all the same to have been truly evil, that we might know more fully that we were saved.

I do not mean to mock, but I do mean to suggest that, however effective, such an approach is wrong. Sin is not only found in our acts of evil and wickedness. If someone asked me, 'What do you know of sin?', I should give the following example (having changed some of the details for obvious reasons). I was some years ago responsible, as chairman of a committee, for appointing a number of people to various jobs. One such person was now coming up to retirement, not only from that position but after some twenty-five years' service to the Church; the tasks had proved greater than imagined, and he had given sacrificially. Before some five hundred people I was to round off the celebration and thanks with the keynote speech of tribute. I prepared it well and delivered it: possibly I did better than anyone else would have done, but somehow I failed to rise to the occasion. The moment passed, that person left for retirement in another part of the country, and the opportunity to express a community's appreciation never came again. There was sin: I had done my best, whatever that means, and it wasn't good enough. This to me is total depravity: that what I did well nevertheless failed.

Most of us are not murderers, thieves and adulterers. Our lives are not caught up in the exciting viciousness of drug dealing, gun running or wanton excess, for most of us are neither that poor nor that rich. And if we were? Those acts of evil would not appear so, or at least not so clearly evil, from those contexts. Not only is it easier to spot other people's sins, but easier still those from a different society.

Sin, however, is not about other people. Sin, if you like, is a first person singular word. I can talk about it in general terms only from what I know in my own terms. That is why self-examination is not merely a good thing, it is essential; and in such self-examination we have to avoid being distracted by the colourful and exciting sins that happen to other people. Take your models from Al Capone and Don Juan and you risk either complacency, if you acquit yourself of their faults, or self-importance, if you condemn.

Here is the value of learning self-knowledge from the products of study. Colour and excitement are not in evidence. What do we find above all in this examination? Most probably, an overwhelming mediocrity. If, for example, we condemn ourselves for laziness, it is unlikely to be laziness on a grand scale, but simply ordinary. The sins that emerge from the text before us are rarely heroic, but commonly mundane. This is an important truth, for if all grace is from God (as indeed it is), there is a constant temptation to believe, however orthodox our faith, that maybe what makes us special and unique as individuals is not what we do well (for that is of God) but what we do badly.

Sin is ours, and we are at all times tempted to cherish it.

Therefore an exercise that reveals our failings as in no way distinctive nor unique, but rather common, boring and mediocre, is salutary. For this alone is sin capable of forgiveness, that which we regret and of which we are ashamed, not that in which we glory, however perversely.

This may not be grovelling, but it does sound rather depressing. It can be at the very least discouraging, and a good reason why we should not perform this exercise too often, nor too zealously. So then, rather than your most recent sermon, essay, painting or report, for a change take one from a year or two back, something long forgotten. It is easier to put your former self under the spotlight, for, with distance, you can laugh at your foolishness and feel no emotional threat from your idiocy. Who knows, you may also discover something that makes you think, 'Was I really that good? I don't remember.' We should not forget that God offers encouragement as well as condemnation.

The technique is the same. Take a finished piece of work and consider it in itself, not what it might have been, nor what you intended it to be, but what it is. Review it slowly to answer, in as much dispassionate detail as possible, the two following questions, 'What did I do wrong?' and 'Why did I get it wrong?' The technique is one of gaining self-knowledge, but without looking directly at one's self.

This is an exercise in self-examination, but I would not like to leave the impression that the last chapter was all about other people, and this one only about ourselves. If the knowledge we gain is of our sins, as neither heroic nor unique, but rather common and mundane, this offers us knowledge of other people as well, victims of the same temptations and failings.

Chapter 3

Preparing for a Crisis

You are visiting a friend in hospital, or walking to the shops, or sitting in a train. Suddenly and unexpectedly someone grabs hold of you or sits down beside you, begging for a few minutes of your time, and then proceeds to unburden himself of some terrible family problem, or a desire to commit suicide, or just an overwhelming sense of suffering, and then asks you what you think, or what you can do to help, or what is the answer. I agree such an event may be more likely to happen if you are dressed as a member of the clergy, but it may equally be that you have a sympathetic face.

Such are the circumstances, you have at the most ten minutes before that person loses concentration, or someone else disturbs you, or you are called away to an important engagement. A sudden, and for you quite unreasonable, crisis that occurs at a most inconvenient moment. What do you say? What can you say? If you think this is hard, what about a telephone call? When all you are dealing with is a little disembodied voice down a crackling phone line asking for help.

Of course if you had at that moment been quite free of worries of your own or obligations to others, and had all the time in the world; if this unwelcome request had not come when you were feeling worn out and weary; if you could somehow have had a few moments to collect your thoughts, or the time and space to prepare a proper answer . . . But you weren't free of your worries, it didn't happen when you were strong, and you hadn't the time to think or pray. Unfair perhaps, but there was nothing you could do about it.

I have cultivated this model, with all its melodrama, for many years. Instances, or meetings very similar, have occurred many times, though perhaps not as often as I had earlier supposed. Sometimes it was simply a well-rehearsed ploy to elicit sympathy before a request for money, and I have developed a few careful questions of my own. Sometimes it has been a statement, an outburst of anger against God or the world, rather than a true question waiting for an answer now. Sometimes, saddest of all, the person who asks and wants some word of hope or comfort has kept his ears so closed to God that he can no longer hear: no words at all seem to get through.

If such is the case, and it is never certain, this only makes the situation even more difficult and frightening to consider. If many times a cry for help is not as serious as it seems, if I am just not the appropriate person to give that help, if it is not in fact the last chance, and help of whatever kind can safely be left until tomorrow, this only makes the real crisis that much harder to discern. If every time someone stopped you and asked for a word of support, a human soul was to be saved, why, you would make sure you were prepared; but if it is only once in a thousand times, or less, this is actually more difficult and worrying.

Certainly this is a fantasy and an exaggeration. Certainly it could lead to an inordinate sense of your own importance: not everyone who seeks a little comfort is looking to you as their last hope on earth. All the same, a little paranoia keeps one on one's toes. I did not invent this drama; I came across it in the play *The Living Room* by Graham Greene. For years the priest has had the opportunity to pray and prepare, but when the crisis comes in the person of a young woman, he is unready and he fails her and she dies.

There are many crises, great and small, that meet us in our lives, all of which can catch us unawares. I have cultivated this particular image because it is unfair, unforgiving and unforeseeable. If you want to be prepared for injury to a companion, learn first aid; if you are worried about being attacked in the street, learn self-defence; if you are concerned

about your car breaking down, learn engine maintenance
and buy the right tools. Other people's spiritual and mental
problems do not, however, allow for such precise, teachable
responses: they may have no solution, and there is no telling
whether you have given the right answer or not.

What stops the fantasy becoming simply a source of
anxiety is that sometimes it does *seem* as though you were
able to give help to someone who crossed your path by
chance or providence. You may be lucky (if this is the right
word), but you can hardly count on it. As with the unexpected guest or the hungry traveller, you open the cupboard:
either there is sufficient food, or there isn't.

It is rarely possible to know the effects of your words or
the results of your actions. Very rarely are clues given. A
'thank you' may only be politeness; indeed the other person
or people may not realize until much later whether you were
a vessel of grace and wisdom, or a waste of time. There is
nothing you can do, when such a crisis or test arrives, but
bring out from what you have in store: it will be either bread
or a stone.

What is an exam? An unfair, irksome, old-fashioned means
of judging intellectual attainment? Should they be got rid of
in favour of fairer means of assessment? No. Exams are a
fine form of spiritual discipline, an exquisite training for real
life. They are that sudden crisis, that moment of testing,
which can strip bare our illusions and show us our real
worth. I am not arguing that students must enjoy the
prospect of examinations, but that we can see in them a
means of training and self-knowledge. They may have been
traumatic at the time, but the memory of them is useful.

School exams remain the paradigm, but as I tried to show
in the last section, real life has its parallels, crises in which
our abilities are indeed put to the test and examined. Let me
add another more formal example, a job interview: it is not
unlike an oral examination in the brevity of the allotted time

and its unfair, unexpected questions. Again, suppose that your boss asks you to write a quick paper on some aspect of the firm's procedures by the next morning: your promotion prospects may depend on the outcome.

Life is not always fair. I am not trying to justify existing teaching practices, but rather to illustrate that we are stuck with one or another form of 'exam' all our life. Our school examinations remain, in their clarity and simplicity, a valuable form of training. For that is their usefulness, not as an academic assessment but as spiritual training.

This is an important change in perspective. The exam is not a trivialization of the real body of school work, nor is it merely the stick or sanction imposed on the laziness of fallen human nature. It is the lynch pin of a style of study, whose discipline sharpens the mind, breaks down our illusions of cleverness, and mirrors the real world. What we have to offer of value is what we *can* produce under pressure and constraint, not what we *could* produce under the best of all possible conditions, at a time and in circumstances of our own choosing.

There is real value in constraint. It is a necessary part of all Christian prayer and spirituality, which is at its best in, and dealing with, the real world. This includes the long and important tradition of the cloistered life, the study of prayer in a monastic setting far from the cares of the world; this has not been from a hatred of God's creation, but as a contribution towards it. The justification for the monastic life, even the most enclosed, has not been the good it does the monk or the nun, but the good it does the Church and the world. Similarly, a university is established with its ivory tower, separated from the cares and busyness of ordinary life, for the good of the nation and beyond, not for itself and its professors.

A deeper look at monasteries shows that where constraints such as earning a living or looking after a family have been removed, others are imposed, such as the hours of prayer or the rule of obedience. We need constraints if we are to produce anything of worth. The same lesson has been shown in the arts: much of what has been created in this century is transitory and of passing worth, precisely because it has thrown off the constraints of former centuries but found nothing with which to replace them; the discovery of a different set of constraints has been one of the challenges for the artist in recent decades. So too in sport, what can be achieved by waiting for perfect conditions is far less regarded next to the big race or match, set beforehand at a precise time and place, which then imposes its own demands on the training and preparation.

There is, however, a problem in the nature of a constraint, in that if we are to use it to our advantage, we must accept it, and yet it may also be a genuine injustice and therefore unacceptable. The most notorious example in Christianity is that of slavery, an inhumanity civilized people no longer regard as in any circumstances permissible; and yet in New Testament times, Paul, aware of the urgency of the gospel proclamation and believing in the imminent return of Christ, saw it only as a constraint, to be endured with humility.

We cannot, however, simply make up our own constraints, free of moral objections. This is one of the problems faced by contemporary artists: you cannot create constraints. There is no possibility of gaining a real and positive benefit unless there is a real and negative limitation. It would be wrong to explain away the pain and the frustration, the injury and the loss which may be caused by the constraints we face, simply because we cannot find a way of using them to advantage. Illness can teach patience, humility and compassion, but it is not to be sought for that reason, nor for any other; indeed it would most probably not be effective if it was so sought, for as I have just remarked, we cannot invent our own constraints.

Escaping or accepting, using or removing the constraints of our lives is a very real predicament. This is why the exam model is so useful. For these are sudden crises of constraint that simply happen: they are as it were upon us before we have the time to question them, or chafe against the yoke. The limitations and unfairness are not clearly delineated in the present, where they can become the subject of discussion, rebellion or modification, but lie somewhere in the future. Perhaps at its simplest life is just like that. Whatever we think or do, we are going sometimes to be taken by surprise, and put on the spot.

So take yourself back and remember what it was like, sitting at a desk in a large school hall at the beginning of an examination. That the time is insufficient for what you have to write is perhaps the easiest constraint to bear, because it applies to everyone equally – well, not quite, because some people have the unfair advantage of being able to write faster than you can. The topics chosen and the form of the questions, they don't seem quite fair to your particular areas of knowledge. Worst of all is the fact that you are feeling ill, you are going down with 'flu (you think), yet no one is prepared to take that into consideration. Such excuses and complaints may be real (and how real they felt at the time!), but they are quite irrelevant, they are not part of the terms of the exam. Outsiders set the rules and conditions, and that's how it is. Life is like that, and it is unfair.

What is the solution? The last two chapters were concerned with specific skills and techniques. This chapter offers nothing as precise, more a particular vision of the future. How does this affect what we do in the present?

If the exam is the goal, then our study now does not have any real worth in itself; it is not the accumulation of knowledge, the steady climbing of a ladder, it is simply preparation, of no real significance until it is put to the test. Study, and prayer, is preparation.

Preparation for what? I have taken exams as the basic model, from which I constructed the picture with which I began this chapter. I simply share it as mine; it has no special value. It is important that you develop your own. One of the simplest and most widespread is that of the unexpected visitor, the person who will suddenly, unannounced, knock on the door and who must be invited in. Because of him, many people living on their own know why they must keep the house tidy and clean and keep the kitchen and larder stocked and prepared.

I call it a fantasy because it goes so much further than the facts suggest, in the age of telephones and late shopping. It is almost a tradition, passed down from mother to daughter: it is far more than a simple expectation, it is rather a discipline of living. Then there is the other popular exhortation always to wear clean underwear in case you get run over by a bus. Again, it is slightly fantastic, but it fosters a discipline of dress; it shares the same vision of the need for preparedness.

You have created and developed your exam model. Now, how do you prepare? You would be foolish to trust to luck. There is a fair expectation that what will be asked of you will be unexpected and unreasonable. Therefore . . . ?

Therefore you must prepare for any eventuality. One needs an active, not a passive, approach to learning: one needs to learn rather than merely be taught. Once again, learning a foreign language provides a good example. Phrase books are undoubtedly useful, but it would be a dangerous approach simply to learn a whole collection of phrases. In theory the wide and careful selection should cover every normal eventuality in the course of a summer holiday, but of course it never works out like that, and situations never present themselves as neatly as one would wish. Only by setting out to learn the language itself, picking up words and phrases that may not appear immediately useful, will it be possible to converse at even the simplest level.

It means that we must work and study harder than we might be inclined to, but at least we know why. And we know, since all our study is but preparation for the unexpected, that nothing we may learn is unnecessary. Because we cannot tell what will or will not be needed, when we are put to the test there is a usefulness in anything we may acquire by way of knowledge or understanding.

In the recent study, or science, of chaos and its laws and patterns, there has been one idea of particular appeal to the popular imagination (it is the example universally quoted in newspaper articles), that the beating of the wings of a butterfly in South America can effect or set off a hurricane in Texas. Not that it *will*, which is absurd, but that it *could*, that the various factors that effect the weather are so interlocked in such a complex manner, that no movement of air is of itself too small to be significant. Nothing is too distant or too small to be excluded from the pattern of cause and effect.

Odd bits of knowledge, or thought, or understanding do not therefore accumulate as separate facts useful only for a general knowledge quiz, but can be fitted together and prove of value in quite unexpected areas. Not that they will (people who are good at quizzes are not necessarily wise), but that they can. Understanding, as opposed to the simple memorizing of facts, is never wasted; it is a quality not an object, and who can ever know when or how it may prove of value in quite another area of human enquiry?

What has this to do with the life of prayer? If we wish to learn how to pray, it is as preparation for the possible crises that may happen upon us in the future. Its value cannot be counted in the present, when we have prepared ideal conditions, but when it is put to the test. 'I pray when I want to', I am often told; it may be all rather too easy when *you* want to, when you have set aside the time, found a conducive place, chosen the style or subject of your prayer, and are feeling well-disposed towards God and his children.

Let us say you go on retreat and follow a course of prayer laid down by the conductor. You have the peace and quiet, your food and worldly needs are being looked after by others, you have the support of other Christians; you have nothing else to worry about, only to pray. You follow the instructions, you make progress, you feel (surely not unreasonably) closer to God; you end the retreat feeling, you might say, a better Christian. It is not however at this moment that you pass the exam and gain your merit badge. What you feel at this point is largely irrelevant, if this learning of prayer was but preparation. Preparation for what? Who knows, but when you are back in the ordinary world, have come down from your cloud, and are once more assailed by the old doubts and failings, when you seem to have fallen back to where you were before you started, then, perhaps, the true value of what you learned may emerge.

If prayer is a preparation, like study, then one cannot afford to keep it in a narrow confine. Mystical prayer, as many adolescents know, can be practised to an extraordinary degree. Forget the dullness of church services and the awkwardness of public gatherings, take the works of St John of the Cross and follow his instructions. With time and application and many hours of solitude, you may develop a depth of contemplative prayer far beyond that of anyone around you. Is this real prayer? I doubt it. It may feel marvellous; others may envy your powers of concentration; but it is unlikely to face any real testing.

Then there is what a colleague once called 'the Good Samaritan syndrome' – if a preacher were free to choose his own text for his sermon Sunday by Sunday, how often would he choose the parable of the Good Samaritan, along with other 'nice' bits such as the Christmas stories or the Resurrection, ignoring (perhaps unconsciously) the difficult passages of Christ's teaching. The Church sets before us the comprehensive discipline of the Christian year and the lectionary precisely to prevent us picking and choosing to our own disadvantage.

'I've never tried it, because I don't like it.' We may laugh at this statement, but something of it is true for all of us. We do not naturally choose, in study or in prayer or in life, what appears to us to be dull and boring, but if we have an understanding of crisis and our need to prepare, we more readily submit to the discipline. To have a clear reason why one should seek out what is new or different or difficult, and to have a strong motive that can overrule inertia, is invaluable.

It is not enough to work hard and learn more. If we are to prepare material for the unknown crisis, it must be ordered. This can sound very daunting and intellectual, but it is not always difficult. We do not create order out of nothing by the sheer power of our own intellect. We observe, if we can, the order of the world. Much of this is of course done in the discussion and argument of study itself, but how do you do your own ordering, relating the events and experiences and thoughts to your life and your self? How do you order your mind?

One persuasive explanation for the purpose of dreams is that they are, at least in part, the means by which the unconscious orders, re-orders and tries to make sense of what has happened to the conscious mind. This bizarre shuffling around of the pieces, in no apparent order, helps to bring them together into a coherent pattern. Organized daydreaming can work very effectively – letting the experiences and emotions and frustrations of waking life float around and re-order themselves in a different pattern entirely. A solution rarely arises immediately, but a day or two later, one hitherto vague idea or another may suddenly become clearer.

Some part of one's prayer should follow this style: to lay the various events and worries and ideas before the Lord, and try to let them float around, without seeking too hard to grasp at a solution. How can one tell whether this has anything to do with prayer? There is the difficulty; there is no answer, but some prayer at least is definitely about *not* asking God for things.

What we are trying to do is to gather our understanding in such a form that it can move effectively in whatever direction it is needed. It is always a sad occasion when a friend loses his or her faith; certainly there is more involved than we can comprehend, but one model does seem common, namely that a question was posed by bereavement, say, or illness, in a form for which that person was unprepared, and the faith cracked. It is foolish to say to oneself, 'I have faith' or 'I have knowledge' if one does not know what new question may suddenly reveal it to be inadequate: a faith untested may not yet be faith.

To take an example from the last chapter, it is important if we are to know the salvation and forgiveness of God that we know ourselves to be sinners. If we see our sins as vile, monstrous manifestations of evil, we are more inclined to receive God's justification as wholly and completely the gift of grace. To be thus born again is to move from darkness to light, with no shadow of grey; such a Christian is armed against the forces of the devil, but what about the trivial, niggling failures of everyday life? Could it not be (and I do not invent this example) that such a Christian might fall away through nothing greater than a craving for chocolate? Prepared for a full-scale war, only to be derailed by petty vandalism.

The task is both to impose order and to let it be imposed. The subtlety of that balance is probably beyond us, and there is no right answer. This is one of the gifts of the Psalms, and one of the reasons why the Church has always had them as the central part of its cycle of daily prayer. They both impose the order of God's law, commands and truth, upon our understanding of life, and allow it to emerge, through the meditative, reflective repetition of the well-known phrases. They are by turns our words and God's words.

Prayer as preparation. It may be dull, it may at times seem like hard work, it may seem to be leading nowhere, but it does have one supreme advantage over the 'I only pray when I need to' approach, namely that when you need to, you won't have to, because you will have done it before.

When life is truly difficult, when major decisions have to be made and great suffering to be endured, when every ounce of your mental and physical strength is called upon, do you then, over and above the overwhelming demands and competing claims of the immediate crisis, do you then have the time or the energy to begin to pray? It seems unlikely. That is why you prayed, day by day, week by week, when you had no particular need to; so that when you really need the help it gives, it is there already.

Chapter 4

Accepting Imperfection

It is of course hard to imagine, but what would you do if you read a book that was perfect, that you knew to be perfect, and furthermore you understood it? What could you do, if the argument, the theory and the description were all complete, coherent and without flaw – quite simply the Truth, the Whole Truth, and nothing but the Truth.

What could you do? In a sense, nothing. You have just to accept it. You cannot put it into different words, view it from a different perspective, question the emphasis here or there, for in each case, whatever you do, you could only end up at a worse point than where you started. You cannot improve on perfection: any alteration leads downhill, away from the truth.

Perfection is a problem for imperfect mortals. 'No man can see God and live' (Exodus 33.20) not merely because we would be destroyed by his awesome majesty and blinded by inexpressible light, but also because we would be frozen by his eternal perfection, unable to move mentally or physically. Difficult as it may be to imagine, this is a fundamental doctrine for our spiritual life, a key to the truth of the incarnation and our understanding of prayer.

We need imperfection to approach the truth. Not errors, faults and mistakes, but something less than perfection that we can get hold of, that allows us to grasp whatever it is we are dealing with.

The Bible is the Word of God. It is true that scholars have discovered and analysed any number of errors of language, calculation, geography and history, but these are

not relevant one way or the other. As the persistent existence of fundamentalists shows, one can simply ignore all
these conclusions or deny them. If the Bible is the Word of
God and the Word of God to humanity, then it can show us
the deliberate ('God-given') imperfection that enables us to
hear it.

The Psalms show this clearly. Part of the Word of God,
they are also, more obviously than any other book, the words
of ordinary people, the forms of song and prayer to be used
by men and women in speaking to God. In praise and
thanksgiving and confession and meditation, here are the
words for us to use; and yet are they not also full of quite
unusable material?

It is *because* they are so clearly imperfect that the Psalms
have been so central and so important to Christian prayer
and worship. Each worshipper and each congregation is
compelled to work at and work with the material offered, to
make it relevant and morally acceptable, whether it is as
simple as excluding the final verse of Psalm 137:

> a blessing on anyone who seizes your babies
> and dashes them against a rock;

or as subtle as the mental adjustment needed to understand
Psalm 15.4:

> who despises the vile man,
> but honours those who fear the Lord

in a manner that accords with charity and courtesy,
or . . . the list goes on.

There is no official commentary or bowdlerization whatever, no officially approved improvement. In my twenties I
devised a pocket prayer book for my own use when travel-
ling; in it I included carefully edited portions of the Psalms,
that excluded the 'nasty' bits, avoided the hints of self-right-
eousness, and removed the archaisms such as the 'tents of
Kadesh'. Whether successful or not, it was a worthwhile
exercise in prayer, but fortunately the Church as a whole has
never attempted such editing.

Suppose it had, and had succeeded; or suppose the original was perfect, leaving no room for any editing or improvement. What could we do? We could do no more than repeat them. Could we, in all humility, reflect upon them? Could we in addition offer to God our own prayers, our own hymns? Would they not be second best, a step back from the prayer and worship we have been given by God himself? The Psalms may, at times, be an embarrassment or a source of frustration, but the very imperfections that annoy us are also the key to our ability to use them to speak to our God, to draw closer to him. Were they perfect, we would be frozen in submission.

Take another example, unencumbered with moral problems; one of the most vividly presented personalities of the Bible is the prophet Jeremiah, who preached (it would seem) in the last years of the Kingdom of Judah, through the two sieges of Jerusalem and into the early years of exile. The long book that bears his name is full of intense, personal expressions of his sufferings, and accounts of the struggles of his rejected ministry. We may feel that we know him more intensely than any other person in the Old Testament, even including David.

Yet, it is impossible to reconstruct his life or to be sure that any one event truly occurred as described, even though we already have a clear history of Judah at this time, from the final chapters of 2 Kings. I say 'impossible' because although scholars have tried, none has succeeded completely, nor even gained general, let alone universal, agreement.

It is as though on completing this major work of history, poetry and preaching the editor accidentally dropped all the pages (he would, it is true, have been using a scroll, but no matter) and was unable or unwilling to put them all back in the correct order. Even more astonishing are the shorter books of Ezra and Nehemiah, of much simpler literary form: surely these chapters could be rearranged back into the 'correct' historical order? They cannot be. Why not? Even this is hard to tell, but it is a striking fact that the apparent tangle cannot be unravelled.

Why did God allow his Word to be so irreversibly confused? Because, had we been offered a complete, consistent and 'perfect' history, it would have remained forever just that, a history. Moving, inspiring, teaching, but relegated to the past, to another age, outside of ourselves. It is because both texts are so imperfect as literature and history that we are forced to get inside them, to work at them, and to struggle with the meaning, that they become for us, even generations later, the means to hearing the Word of God. Improve the text and the voice of God would grow dim.

It seems best to describe first the value of imperfection, rather than its inevitability. Too vivid a sense of our own failings can lead so easily to apathy, whereas the hope that those failings may have a usefulness ought to be a source of encouragement.

Our own efforts at prayer or at study will inevitably be inadequate, whether public or private. We do not need to be told this, and there is therefore a strong temptation not to finish or complete what it is that we have begun, precisely for that reason. If judged, our effort will be found wanting; therefore, we say to ourselves, let us stop short of the point of judgement. Occasionally this can be an effective expression of our limitations; more often it is a laziness or want of courage.

The advantage of formal study is that we are required to complete and present a piece of work: stopping half-way is not allowed. So let us consider it, an essay, a translation, a programme, or one of the informal equivalents, a painting, a meal, a speech. What is this particular exercise of prayer?

It may seem similar to the exercise of confession, as a careful examination of a finished piece of work, but it is much less precise. What we are looking for this time are not errors and mistakes that stand in need of correction, but, more vaguely, for what cannot be corrected but acts nevertheless as a limitation.

To say something meaningful is not to say something else; this is fairly obvious. But since so much of what we wish to convey is by implication, and so much of what is received is by inference, it is impossible to avoid the disjunction between the two: what you hope to imply is not always what is inferred. We only have to listen to someone, desperate to avoid their audience making the wrong inference, qualifying every statement and then qualifying every qualification, to sense how impossible it is to guarantee that someone will always understand exactly what you mean.

Confusing, isn't it? It is perhaps helpful to imagine a discussion. You are an observer, listening to, say, half a dozen people seeking to formulate a conclusion; not an argument or debate, but several heads together searching for a solution. Differences of emphasis, different perspectives, even disagreements, all help to build up a fuller picture than one person could achieve alone.

But while six people may give a description that is close to being complete, it is less likely to be consistent. One person may put forward something more consistent, but less likely to be complete. There is in other words, or so it seems, an inherent imperfection in whatever form is used. It is not an error, to be corrected; it is just how it is. There is advantage and disadvantage in whichever form is taken.

It is this degree of imperfection that one seeks to understand in this particular exercise of prayer. Concentrate on the part of your argument or presentation that seems to be the neatest, the most convincing, the most informative. Success here suggests a lack of success elsewhere. If your grasp of the details is superb, perhaps the overall view is weak; if the head is clear, perhaps the heart was not moved; if you have solved one problem, you may have ignored another; and so on.

It is not an easy task, for as in confession, we are most definitely not asked to grovel, nor to acknowledge our general failure and unworthiness. But unlike confession, we are not searching here for precise faults which may then be corrected. What we are looking for now is neither precise nor necessarily correctable.

To understand and describe the limitations of one's presentation is an important exercise in its own right. It is as though, while being tempted by the praise and congratulations of others to believe in their assessment, you are trying to add a final rider, that it is not complete, that there may be weaknesses, that here or here there may be an incoherence that others, with a different perspective, will have to tackle and perhaps solve. It is not easy either to want to do it or to be able to.

It is no different in prayer itself, this limitation of commitment. The temptation is to take a middle-of-the-road, lowest-common-denominator, all-things-to-all-men approach to God and our relationship with him. Popular perhaps, but pointless, for whichever road the Spirit leads us, it will inevitably have its own limitations. Speaking in tongues or contemplating in silence, liturgical dance or the traditional prayer book: we cannot do all of it, all of the time.

If we actually *do* anything, as opposed to just thinking about it, we are caught by imperfection. Wisdom lies in seeking to know this and understand it, and then to perceive its worth.

In the Jewish tradition, more strongly than the Christian, the Sabbath, as the day of rest, is understood as a foretaste of heaven, when the work imposed on fallen man ceases and we share briefly the calm, peace and joy of the heavenly realm. There is a Rabbinic tradition which develops the understanding further: *if*, just once, everyone kept the Sabbath perfectly, no work intruded, no busyness marred the calm, and nothing broke the peace, then that Sabbath rest would continue, the new week would not begin – there would be no need, for heaven once truly found could not be lost.

While the weeks succeed each other, it is clear that we have not yet arrived, we are still journeying. To stop too long on that pilgrimage would either be an illusion or a mistake or a failure.

An aside. There is one area of ignorance that will guarantee imperfection, that ought to keep us humble and waits to trip us up if we are not. However well you know your subject, however focused your vision, there will always be details on the edge, on the periphery of your vision, that you believe you understand, but that others know better. I spoke of a 'Rabbinic tradition'; in fact I only heard tell of it at second hand, and in this lonely parish have no means of checking its source; I believe I speak correctly, but I cannot remove a lurking suspicion that someone else knows better, and will mock the clumsiness of my ignorance. Of course you can rigorously confine your area of study, but it is unlikely you will have anything worth saying unless you stick your neck out just a little further than is safe. You cannot ensure that all you say will always be correct.

Our life is a journey. It is worth pausing to consider this statement: it is a good example of what this chapter is about. The Church as a whole, from its most authoritative documents to its most popular spiritual writing, has over the last few decades rediscovered and re-emphasized this truth. I don't suggest we deny this particular perception, nor belittle the achievements of understanding it has encouraged, nor question our commitment to it as a guiding principle. And yet. What aspect of the truth is correspondingly being ignored? What correction will be made by a later generation? I do not know. If I did, I would change my argument. All I can note is this sense of imperfection, that a crucial truth may not be the whole truth.

Our life is a journey. Therefore, we cannot have the last word. Nor will we hear it, this side of heaven. Thus we should seek to present the products of our study and prayer in such a manner that we do not imply, nor believe that they are, the last word. Equally, when in prayer we hear the voice of God, it will be the truth, but not the end of it.

Does this mean that we should be timid? No, rather the reverse. One of the best pieces of advice I received as a young curate concerned preaching: 'Unless you veer towards heresy, you will never preach the gospel.' Unless one can push the argument and its implication towards an unortho-dox conclusion, one cannot grasp the power and strength of orthodoxy itself.

To say only what is true, only what cannot be miscon-strued, is on the whole to remain with platitudes and truisms: they are not false, but they do not generally inform and teach, or draw the hearer towards a greater truth. I am not quite sure how I would describe the results of acting upon that advice. It is perhaps something to do with the fact that a hearer of the word will rarely go quite as far in the argu-ment or the passion as the speaker, who has spent so much more time thinking about it; so that you need to go two steps in a sermon to help the congregation to go one step.

We must not be timid. But what are the implications of this exhortation to courage? This is both the great problem and the great glory of Anglicanism. Joseph Butler, Bishop of Durham in 1750, was one of the very great Anglican preachers. He asked that on his death all his unpublished papers should be destroyed, and, unusually, they were. I have a volume of his complete works, sermons, books and letters – everything in 600 pages. He was not simply a great theo-logian, of interest to theologians, but his *Fifteen Sermons* is one of the greatest texts of moral philosophy in the whole history of philosophy.

By contrast, the German theological tradition is not shy of words. Martin Luther's collected works amount to some fifty-five volumes, Karl Barth's *Church Dogmatics* alone was translated into English in thirteen volumes, while more recently Karl Rahner's *Theological Investigations* has now surpassed twenty volumes. Of the two approaches, clearly the Germans are closer to the mainstream: consider the sheer mass of writing from the two great Doctors of the Church, Augustine and Thomas Aquinas.

Faced with the ultimately impossible task of knowing and

describing the truth, which approach is correct? There must be merit in the relentless and rigorous pursuit of every last detail, and due authority is generally given to such heavyweight thinkers, but I would plead strongly (well I would, wouldn't I?) for Anglican reserve. If learning is judged by content alone, wisdom is judged not only by the content but also by the quality of the writing, a quality that can be lost under too many words.

If life is a journey, then study in its widest sense is a discussion. The ability *not* to say everything, but to allow others to take on the search or debate, is a quality of wisdom. You are, let us imagine, putting forward your point of view: your hearers do not seem to have grasped it: do you repeat it, draw out some of the implications, add the qualifications, a further example or two, and then put the whole into different words? Do you go on at such length that others become restless, cease listening and merely wait for you to stop, before someone else has their say? I acknowledge, to my shame, that I have done this all too often.

Thoroughness is not wicked; it is just so often self-defeating. Possibly in the top academic circles it is what is called for, but that is hardly relevant to most of us. The content may be important, but so too is the quality of the speaking, the writing or the painting. By 'quality' I do not mean a particular style, but the ability to combine a passionate conviction for the theme with a reserve that does not seek to have the last word, nor underline every implication, but to pass on that task to the hearer.

The great medieval cathedrals are, as the guide books will tell you, slightly askew – the nave does not properly align with the chancel. There is a common tradition (in many cultures) in the large scale public arts of architecture and decoration to include a deliberate imperfection in the design, so that the artist or craftsman cannot be accused of trying to emulate God; however the mistake is often so small it has to be pointed out, which rather weakens the purpose of it.

Most of the great cathedrals go further: the imperfection is immediately obvious, even troubling, for they seek to represent the broken body of Christ. Here is an imperfection that works powerfully, suggesting in stone that even Christ as Son of Man cannot be shown to us in his perfection, but in his broken state upon the cross. The architectural imperfection is often further increased by changes in the plans while building, the ravages of fire and war and later rebuilding, failed hopes, shortened spires and financial compromises.

I sometimes wish that the original plans for, say, Lichfield or Chartres, had been fulfilled; and then again I don't, for it is the richness of the whole with all its faults that works most strongly. None of these great buildings are complete or consistent, and so they do not simply stand there, but seem to move, and lead, the pilgrims to something beyond themselves. The sense of what might have been as one studies the dissonance of styles, the repairs and the additions leads one to imagine what it could or should have been like, and so to one's own vision of how to glorify God, and so to God himself.

Like cathedrals, like Gospels. An irreverent suggestion: if God is so smart, why did he not work it so that there was only one complete Gospel, and not four that do not quite fit together; or indeed if the Church were smart, why did it not accept the harmony of the Gospels devised by Tatian around the year 150, instead of ignoring it into oblivion?

A single Gospel would indeed be easier, but would it be a Gospel? No; with the passage of centuries, it would have become a biography of Jesus (hagiography perhaps), but not a Gospel as we understand it. God is wise: he knew that four Gospels, *including* all the difficulties they present, could together achieve what a single one, or a harmonization, never would.

Here is the central figure of our faith, his life, his teaching, and his Passion, and we are not given a clear, straightforward account! It seems most unfortunate. This is not, however, a failing of the disciples, but a gift of God. At even the simplest, most untutored reading, we are faced with the seeming inconsistencies, and at once drawn into . . . a challenge, a process, a journey? We have to work with the texts, and move with them and beyond them to Jesus himself.

That is what a Gospel is for − to bring us to Jesus. One alone would have stood as a complete, consistent, sacred monument; with four none can claim priority, and none can be ignored. Largely because of the imperfections, they have to be read and re-read and studied and thought about and questioned. And thus it is that they give us Christ.

This necessary imperfection is not the same as error; therefore scholarly criticism cannot offer a solution. Many inconsistencies can, it is true, be harmonized, but that does not of itself bring us closer to Christ. It is a useful exercise to search out the most probable sequence of events in the arrest, trial and crucifixion of Jesus − useful, because it presents us with a range of problems, possibilities and understandings that a simple reading of the Gospel accounts might not give us.

In my youth, the most popular paperback re-presentation of the Passion was *The Trial of Jesus of Nazareth* by S. G. Brandon. Jesus the revolutionary. To the uninformed, it was strikingly new, exciting and convincing. What then was the appropriate reaction? For several friends, it simply became *the* gospel substitute, superseding the clumsy, biased versions of the Bible. They gained a clear, consistent history of Jesus the man, at the expense of the gospel itself, the presentation of Jesus the Son of God. It all made sense, but what did it mean? If Jesus were only a son of man, we would indeed be better off with a good, full biography; it is because he is also the Son of God that a biography is impossible.

If the perfection resides in God and his Son, then it must not reside in any presentation of him: it is as simple as that.

It is a common mockery of Christianity that the New Testament is such second-rate literature. Listen to classical scholars on the subject of New Testament Greek: it positively makes them squirm, it is so crudely inferior and inelegant. Quite so! That's the whole point. As Paul himself said, he was no orator, he had no command of words; isn't this why God chose him, for in his weakness he laid bare the wisdom of God?

These are difficult ideas; what then of the technique, the practical connection between study and prayer, the lesson to be learned? There is nothing as straightforward as there is in the exercise of confession, but something nonetheless.

The perfection we seek to understand or to portray is in God: therefore our work or prayer should never seek nor claim for itself that perfection. It is a means to an end, or as I would prefer to say, a journey towards a goal. It must show two things – movement and heuristic. I shall explain.

By movement I mean that your piece of work, whether an essay or a painting or whatever, does not seek to have the last word, to stop dead the argument or exploration. Any result of study seeks to be both consistent and complete. These aims depend on each other – a thesis could not claim to be complete unless it was also consistent, nor can we tell if it is consistent until it is complete. And yet, as one pushes nearer to the edge, as one hopes to advance to the limit, they are also in conflict.

If you are in any way pushing at the frontiers of knowledge or perception (however modestly), you can move close to being complete or consistent, but not both. Aim at completeness, and you will gather a number of loose ends; aim for consistency, and you will have to leave them out. Your purpose, your style or your background will tend to push towards one goal more than the other. It seems to me – and this is only an observation – that Christians, when writing on spiritual matters, tend towards completeness more than towards consistency. I suppose this is to do with the vastness of God and his creation.

The task, therefore, on completing a piece of work, is to seek to discover which aim predominates, which goal is the closer to being achieved, and therefore which fails the more. Where, in other words, lies the inevitable weakness?

It may even be possible to mark it, to tell your reader, real or imaginary, where you yourself may have fallen short and where he or she may be able to pick it up and carry it further. I said 'movement' because that seems the crucial image, that your work is part of a larger process, a relay race, a journey that will continue long after you are gone.

Is that depressing? No, the reverse is. Suppose you really did manage to have the last word? That subject would then die, it would have no further life, and the product of all your study would be at best a monument, at worst forgotten.

This has nothing to do with leaving your work unfinished, stopping short of a conclusion or ignoring difficulties. To return to Bishop Butler, his two sermons 'On Compassion' are the most profound and successful treatments of the subject in existence; but the result is not to close off that subject, but to open it out: one comes away from reading them wanting to understand more of compassion and to know it more in oneself. He opens not closes the subject. How he achieves this is not, most definitely not, easy to imitate.

It is the gift of wisdom to discover more *and* leave more to discover. It may help to consider what not to do. There is a genre of academic literature, with books entitled 'Prolegomena . . . ' or 'Thoughts Towards . . .' or such like, that is a very deliberate attempt only to have the first word, not to say everything, to leave the task to others. Admirable? Not a bit of it; it is more usually the height of hubris, a combination of egotism and laziness that would nowhere else be tolerated, for the authors do not seek to advance a subject or to struggle with a problem, but rather to lay down the ground rules, the methodology and the terminology, to bind the hand of future generations of scholars, so that no matter where they move nor what conclusions they reach, our hero X remains for ever the father (or mother) of this particular branch of academic study.

Do not seek the last word, nor the first word, but accept your part in the middle of an enterprise larger than yourself. If you have stood on the shoulders of others, pray that others will stand on yours.

Heuristic. An awkward word. 'User friendly' might be better, but it is more than that: it is to do with placing the stress on the learning, rather than the teaching. What matters, in all wisdom, is what is learned rather than what is taught: therefore design your work so that others may learn from it, whether you remain to teach it or not.

There are some pictures, and I can think of a particular artist's water-colours of northern England, that are so technically superb and so carefully balanced that they almost demand the label 'perfect'. Exquisitely beautiful, and yet, we say, they are cold. I don't think this is the right word, for it has nothing to do with the warmth of the colours used: it is the fact that we are not drawn in to them, to learn more about this farmhouse in Upper Swaledale: it is as though the picture is telling us, rather than allowing us to enter it and to discover for ourselves.

The task, therefore, is to question whether your work is, in this sense, cold, whether it excludes your reader, whether it is so technically superb it has no need for a reader. Does it enthuse or does it intimidate? Does it open up the subject, or close it down? It is hard to unlearn the truth and hard for teachers to imagine themselves the student.

There is, though, a quality of imperfection that provides a door by which the viewer or reader may enter. It is this that we should seek to include in all our work. It is of course easier to describe the opposite case. I have always said, and meant it, that I never want to be a good vicar. I had an indirect experience of one in an earlier parish. He was the archetypal Good Vicar, charming, spiritual, intelligent, kind, generous, hard-working . . . . The church was full, the congregation alive, the parish thriving. And then he left. So did two-thirds of the congregation, and nothing was ever the same again. Perhaps they had been drawn into the church by his goodness, and finding him so near perfect (so it seemed) they never went through him to Christ himself; they worshipped the vicar, not his Master, and when he left they felt hurt and betrayed and implacably sad.

It is quite possible to be so brilliant that one dazzles anyone who follows. Fortunately, for most of us this is not a problem: the risk of being too perfect is merely hypothetical. So much the better; we shall not receive the plaudits of the crowd, but maybe, stumblingly, *because* we are so inadequate, we shall be able to help others on the journey to the truth.

Chapter 5

The Journey So Far

I have outlined four exercises that can be applied to a subject of study irrespective of its content. The first teaches us how to listen, the second self-examination (in particular of our failings), the third prepares us for the future, and the fourth prevents us seeking perfection. The first two are formal and precise, and can be undertaken even by those who do not understand a wider purpose; the second two need an appreciation of the why as well as the how. The first and the third are to be practised while one is studying; the second and the fourth are largely useful after one has completed a particular piece of study.

There are three ways in which these exercises can prove useful. First, as a means of deepening one's prayer by learning from the disciplines of study. Second, as a means of deepening one's most serious areas of study, by applying a discipline of prayer. Third, and this is the most general point, as a means of understanding something of the mystery of the world; whether one calls this prayer or study or neither, it is part of the necessary discipline for gaining wisdom.

These are exercises, which like tools can be used for more than one purpose. The justification for learning a skill is that its application and usefulness will be far wider than that of the original context. In all cases, each experience should be learned in the first form, from study, for it is here that the skill is at its most formal and most impersonal. Once it is learned in its simplest context, each skill can be applied and modified in any other context.

First things first. Have you followed each of the four exercises? There is more to be said, but it would have no real value apart from the exercises. When I say 'done', I mean have you practised them to the point of understanding what they are about, not 'done' as in completed or finished. Once one has grasped the purpose, they cease to be formal exercises, and become simply the way of doing things, the way one studies, or prays, or lives.

'Simply the way one studies'? Perhaps not exactly. There is a subtle difference between 'simply studying' and 'studying with prayer in mind'. The four exercises get progressively more sophisticated, more theological in aspect, and more demanding of an understanding why. A particular perception of the world, ourselves and God begins to emerge.

It is important, however, not to become tied up in doctrines and metaphysics. No particular Christian view of the world is required before we begin to walk the path of wisdom. Wisdom is itself the journey, not the conclusion. When in heaven we shall see God, we shall know him as we are known, and either all will be wise, or none will need wisdom, for our knowledge will be complete.

Wisdom is not best described by its content but by the quality of its perception. Wisdom is indeed a gift from God, the capacity (in part) to see as God sees, to share his perception. How do we put ourselves into the way of receiving this gift? By learning these four skills: of listening, of self-examination, of preparation, and of imperfection.

I cannot quite say that wisdom *is* the acquisition of these four skills, in both prayer and study, and this is not simply because it would be presumptuous. We have always to remember that wisdom is a gift, and that we cannot by our own efforts make ourselves wise. Nor can we by our own efforts make ourselves good, but in both cases we can do something, something significant to possess the quality we desire.

I did not invent these exercises, nor have I described them perfectly. The distinction of four categories is somewhat artificial, though I believe devising further ones would have been more so. There is no value in the exercises beyond their usefulness in acquiring particular skills. Those skills may themselves be poor and inadequate, but until one acquires better, should not be despised.

It would be as well to pause at this stage, to reflect upon these four exercises, and to take some stock of progress thus far, before returning to each in turn, to consider their still wider implications.

Part Two

. . . in stillness,
and in staying quiet,
there lies your strength.

Isaiah 30.15

Chapter 6

Opening Your Heart

The purpose of taking so austere a discipline as learning Greek vocabulary is that its stark simplicity can teach us a particular way of paying attention, of concentrating, of listening to the apparent silence. We hope to learn how to do it, and what it is that we are doing. Once we have grasped the basic skill, we can begin to apply it, to use it in our prayer, and in our life as a whole.

I have spoken of learning New Testament Greek because that is my own experience and one common to many Christians, sharing as we do a common Bible. The Hebrew of the Old Testament is equally effective and likely to prove even more difficult and testing. Any subject can offer the same discipline; the particular merit of a foreign language is that it offers fewer tempting short cuts, it will always involve hard work and it has a solid body of correct answers, provided by texts or people who were born to it.

In considering a subject of study not for its own sake but for its discipline of listening, it is best to take one that you find difficult. What you are good at, what comes easily, is more likely to distract you by the quality and satisfaction of the results. In the same way it is sometimes too easy to listen to someone who speaks well; if everyone told their tale of woe as poetically as the Ancient Mariner we should all be ready listeners. In choosing something less compelling there should nevertheless be some goal you wish to aim at, some reason for the subject for its own sake; there is no merit in masochism.

With sufficient imagination and application, no subject is

beyond the pale. One could envisage an evening class in flower arranging as an excellent opportunity for learning a patient attention to the balance and harmony of nature's colours and forms. There are indeed many books on the art, there are methods to be learned and styles to be followed, but for all that it is not so thoroughly in the hands of academic experts as, say, history or literature. Nor is it likely to come with a set of preconceptions learned at school.

I recently prepared a series of evening classes for the Royal Air Force on 'Wine Tasting and Prayer'; not surprisingly they did not take me seriously, so it never happened. But I like the idea, if one could avoid the inevitable snobbery such subjects attract. Our taste and smell are generally far less trained than our sight and hearing; equally, they are nothing like as intellectualized. If people do come up with weird and wonderful descriptions, it is partly because we all struggle to describe in words what is happening on the tongue. It seemed to me that you would have to listen with quite extraordinary intensity (assuming you are not already an expert) to pick out, analyse and remember so fleeting a sensation.

At first you wouldn't know what you were doing; you would find that sense of panic, such as when you encounter a new type of church service or when someone comes with a problem way beyond your experience. 'How am I going to make sense of anything? Where do I begin?' Then slowly, carefully following the instructions you do not yet understand, more and more would fall into place, something entirely new would begin to emerge. Forget the other people, who may or may not be bluffing, and you would start to recognize, understand and compare tastes and smells you had not even noticed before; you would be listening to something you never believed could in fact be heard.

This can be very exciting indeed. I have only once been to a formal, public wine tasting. One of the wines was a Beaujolais, a Chiroubles to be precise. As I tasted it with careful concentration, I realized that I really could remember the previous year's vintage of the same wine that I had tasted some eighteen months earlier. How on earth could I remember such detail from so tenuous a sensation, so long before? I have no idea, but I knew I had. A wine expert may smile, and would surely have been able to describe far more than I had grasped. But it is not expertise we are after here. It is the fact that stumblingly, ignorantly, we can, with the discipline of study, learn to listen to sounds far below our normal threshold, and unearth details we never knew existed.

I have mentioned painting several times. I took it up only recently, and it is still far too early for me to know if I will ever be any good at it, but it has become one of my principal disciplines of prayer as well as a major pastime. There is clearly more than one such discipline of prayer, as I discovered when I went on a retreat entitled 'Painting and Prayer'. By the time we met for the first evening session it was dark, so in the large conference room we took out paper and pencil and were told as an opener to 'draw a tree – *your* tree'.

'Your tree!' I thought in horror: that's everything I am trying to avoid. I don't want *self*-expression, I want God's tree. This is for me the heart of wisdom, not creating something of one's own, but understanding what is already there. The trouble with 'your tree' is that it is by definition always right, whatever marks you put down on paper; God's tree will demand a lifetime of listening and observation.

There are certainly a whole range of ways in which painting links with prayer. The discipline I am speaking of here is not concerned with self-expression. It may be too harsh to say that it should be avoided at all costs, rather that it is achieved by ignoring completely any desire to express your *self*; there is more than enough out there. In losing self, you will find both your self and expression: search for your self, and you will lose both.

I usually go out into the countryside to paint from nature; the task is set by circumstances, the size of the paper I have carried and the time available, often very short when the weather is bad. There is quite a bit of 'knowledge' to be learned, on mixing colours, judging composition, assessing tonal values and such like, but for the most part it is a question of looking and then describing in form and colour what one sees.

It is important to emphasize that this has nothing whatsoever to do with what is called 'realism'. No particular style of painting is favoured over another; no one style is inherently better than another. If I don't paint abstracts, it is because I wouldn't be skilled enough to know what I was doing. Of course, one's own skill and predilections will suggest a particular style or range of styles, probably very different from that of a friend sitting nearby, but one's goal, and the criteria of judgement, are entirely based on what is out there, *not* on what is in your heart.

Like the Curé d'Ars, I may fail over and over again, but that does not especially matter; what was of value was the time of concentration and the struggle to translate what was there on to paper. It is also a highly enjoyable activity; one is taken out of oneself. In that sense it is more relaxing than many forms of relaxation, even though it does require an effort of will to get started.

I paint because I enjoy it, but analysing it I can see other advantages. I can become so absorbed I fail to notice that I am getting painfully cold, or that the sun has moved round and I am getting sunburnt, or once concentrating hard on a brilliant sunset it was only as I finished that I realized it was almost completely dark. If I could listen to a friend with such absorption, then I would indeed be a good listener.

Any subject can become a form of prayer. The advantage of an austere and difficult one is that the discipline of it is more obvious. We all, however, need encouragement, so my advice would be to take at least one leisure activity you truly enjoy to develop the skill of listening. Something interesting and worthwhile, something that warms the heart.

We saw in Chapter 1 that translating Greek is like car maintenance: there is a solution, so you do not search in vain. But what about listening to people? Or listening to

God? Can we, or should we, expect to find an answer? The answer to that question is both 'Yes' and 'No'. Let me explain.

Whether kneeling in prayer or sitting in a chair listening to your friend pour out her problems, you are in effect asking a question, if you are listening to what God or your neighbour has to say. Listening is questioning. As I described in Chapter 1, if you find the answer, you stop listening. That may sound harsh or even cynical, but it is certain that the context changes, as at the very least a new type of question is asked and the conversation or the prayer alters in character.

To be a good listener is not to provide answers. It therefore follows that Christians, or others with strong convictions, do not necessarily make good listeners. Intelligence or experience are not immediate advantages. You may indeed know the answer to the person's problem or dilemma, or you may feel certain that, in God's world, there must be an answer, but that is of no help to listening.

It may be more helpful to suppose that there may well be no solution, or at least none that you will readily find, so that you have to concentrate on exactly what is being said, with no help or short cuts from your own expertise. So too with God. It is true that some of the saints heard a precise word of God at a precise moment, such as St Francis when he heard the gospel words, 'Go, sell all you have . . .', but it does not follow that we all shall. Perhaps God wants us simply to listen to him.

So do you sit there in total silence as your friend pours out his troubles? Not at all. There *may* be no solution to his problem, but there is clearly an answer to your listening, unspoken question, 'What *is* the problem?' Each of us analyses our experience, consciously or unconsciously; each of us has a memory that selects, omits and re-orders; each of us has a pattern of thoughts and expectations that help us both to understand and to misunderstand what happens to us. If you are listening, you are seeking to get beyond these explanations and elaborations, however valid they may be.

You are trying to find that answer, and you just keep asking the questions; by which I do not mean you pretend you are a professional counsellor or psychoanalyst. It is not the practical details of what you may say, it is the attention you give. It has nothing to do with pastoral skills, but is the practice and discipline of concentration, of waiting for the truth; the ability to carry on waiting despite the distractions of your solutions or the speaker's.

Listening is a very demanding activity: we cannot sustain the necessary level of concentration for long. So it is not surprising that impatience is a common fault, as we snatch at a solution; to ease the strain of paying attention, we rush to a conclusion in order to get on to the next question or the next task.

Impatience may be the principal failing that reduces our ability to concentrate, but it is by no means the only one. Consider boredom. Boredom, ennui, apathy, a lack of interest, a loss of purpose, not only in the subject to hand but in life as a whole, to the point where it can become a clinical illness – depression.

You love your wife or husband more than you love Greek? I am sure you do, but it is precisely for this reason that boredom with a spouse, which must happen in any marriage from time to time, is more difficult to cope with and touches your soul more deeply than boredom with Greek ever will. Is it fair to say that if you cannot defeat it in Greek, you will not defeat it in more complex circumstances? This is rather simplistic; but the thought does sharpen the concentration, and underline the force and scope of the spiritual discipline involved. It is not impossible to imagine someone seeking your counsel who might be so boring and heavy-going as to make even Greek seem preferable.

This may seem rather melodramatic, but it is a useful lesson to recognize, as you struggle with a Greek sentence, that powerful sense of boredom and apathy. You tell yourself that there is no point in translating this passage from a dead language that has already been translated before, but with your spouse it will be different, because that does matter. Probably true, but definitely wrong. Too much is involved in our life to use our life as the only lesson in wisdom.

It is not just boredom you are trying to understand and come to grips with, but all the feelings tied up with it. Such as frustration (with your own failings) or lack of will power (a difficult notion to grapple with) or annoyance (at other people's success) or shame (over your former sloth). A strange activity is introspection, and what a wealth of confusion emerges. Study may provide the handle you need to grasp some of these emotions and feelings.

Here, before this page of Greek, you come face to face with something of your character and your problems, but you can shout and scream and vent your rage without hurting another person, or losing your faith. You can always laugh at yourself; in the end it does not matter that much, it is only a bit of Greek. After half an hour of frustration, you can always get up, go for a walk, have a drink or kick a football.

It is not all frustration, because you will make progress. Consider how you would teach this discipline of concentration to a child, say a ten-year-old beginning to learn French. It would be pointless to try to explain what I have been discussing: the poor child would not understand a word. If you set up a simple, clearly-defined task of translation or speaking, all you could offer, beyond the teaching itself, would be essentially negative encouragement, 'No, don't screw your eyes up . . . Relax, don't worry . . . Take your time, don't rush . . . Think carefully . . .' You cannot properly teach a child *how* to learn French, and yet children do learn; even poor pupils improve and can come to enjoy it.

I thought at one point my whole 'theory' of concentration would be worthless until I could explain how one teaches it to children. Now I find it a matter of real encouragement that part of it does come naturally. Of course there are huge problems and distractions, and teaching children is never easy, but they do learn. And they can listen. Why? Because they are curious; because they are interested; because they have a natural desire to learn. This is the key.

If we seek wisdom, desire must move our heart, a desire for the truth and nothing less. Such desire does not come upon us fully formed, but it can begin very early. Think of young children's insatiable desire for answers to their questions, their fascination for accumulating facts, especially the obscure and irrelevant ones. I believe such a desire is there to be developed, that knowledge and understanding are not unnatural (or merely academic) pursuits.

What is evident is that a desire for the truth, if it is to mean anything, must be a balance between both the general and the particular. We seek both Truth with a capital T and the specific incarnation of the truth, in the text of New Testament Greek or in a painting or . . . A general Truth is of little value if truth is not also found in the innumerable problems and tasks that present themselves to us; and it is in these that we take up or ignore the challenge.

There was a funny little song which I vaguely remember from my childhood that contained the following verse, of modest poetic worth, but sung with a great sense of the singer's own worth and love and courage: 'I'd walk to Timbuktu, if I knew that I'd find you. I'd cross the desert bare, if I knew that you'd be there.' Wouldn't we all! If we *knew* that we would be able to attain our heart's desire, of course we would put in the effort and the struggle and the hard work. Crossing the Sahara may be hard, but if it is guaranteed to be worth the ordeal, we would consider it; but if all that pain and hardship might be a complete waste of time, then the task is immeasurably greater and more daunting. It is the not knowing that saps the resolve; the doubts rise and the fears grow that it will all be useless, and nothing will come of it.

So we tailor our desire to manageable ends, and in the practice and struggle the desire deepens. The vision slowly widens the further we walk, and we are led on by the gifts of truth. Such a gift is enjoyment. Again look at young children, whose early learning tasks, even with today's teaching, seem fearfully dull and repetitive. Yet almost universally they show an enjoyment and enthusiasm for simple facts and skills, whose excitement we ourselves have long since lost.

At a more mature level, it may be awe and wonder. Awe at the greatness of the truth and the strange beauty of God's world, at every level from the cosmos to the quark and what we discover in between. Even, behind the confusing constructions, awe at the richness and complexity of an ancient language like Greek in the hands of Palestinian Jews of the first century, the depth of meaning and suggestion of the mystery of God and the human experience. And even in flower arranging? Yes, it may not happen often, but there can be wonder that a collection of unsuitable twigs and flowers has been made (by you? it doesn't matter) not merely competent, but into something strangely peaceful and beguiling.

And then there is one of the most singular of the gifts, generosity. Singular, because it often comes upon us unawares; our heart opens, despite our conscious thoughts. It has happened that I have been drawn into a fierce and passionate argument with someone of diametrically opposed views; I can leave, angry and frustrated, with the feeling 'What a waste of time!' Yet some days later, after a night or two's sleep, without my thinking about it at all, I suddenly discover that my ideas have changed and grown. Somehow, despite my own intentions and conscious thought, my heart's desire for the truth opened it to receive what I was sure I had rejected.

'Desire for the truth' – if we see this as a feeling of the

mind, it can seem cold, intellectual and laden with a strong
sense of ought and of duty. But its source is in the heart. It
is the heart that *wants* to hear and understand, to be more
and more open to one's self, other people, the world and
God.

Compassion is the great example of this desire, for it is
the supreme gift that teaches us why the truth matters.
Waiting on the lonely shore, before he came to feed the
crowd, the Gospel says of Jesus that 'his heart went out to
them, and he had compassion on them, for they were like
sheep without a shepherd' (Mark 6.34). We may wonder
how it could have been that he could feel compassion for as
many as five thousand men, not to mention the women and
children. How? Because he knew the truth of each one of
their lives; because he had heard every one of their cries.

Chapter 7

Growing in Self-awareness

To know yourself is to know that you sin. But what is there to be learned from a knowledge of one's sins? Following the exercise of Chapter 2, you have begun to learn how to identify what you have done wrong and why you did it. The first lesson, as we saw, is one of realism: we see ourselves not as glorious angels of light fallen from heaven, but in all our dull ordinariness.

The great merit of practising this 'confession of sins' in the context of study is that it happens without intrusive emotion. There is no wailing and gnashing of teeth, no abject humiliation, when re-reading an essay. Perhaps there isn't in church either, but the temptation is present, if only because the wrongs are so much more serious, involve real hurt and injure other people. I may feel shame at what I wrote, but not a fraction of the shame I have felt in deeds of malice against my neighbour. The quiet process that reflects on the meaning of our failings rather than exaggerating them into devouring demons, should lead to two particular virtues, humility and tolerance.

Humility is best understood not as a virtue but as a grace, for none of us can make ourselves more humble, but only place ourselves in a position to receive it as a gift from God. We can do this only with knowledge, knowledge of our true self, for humility, in the Christian tradition, is linked to the truth. If we truly know ourselves (that is, if the understanding of the mind is shared by the heart) then we would be humble, with no specific, additional moral quality of modesty or self-abasement.

If humility is a grace, its behaviour is gracious. We can learn much from recognizing this graciousness in the actions of others. In our own lives, we draw nearer to it not by considering our successes but our failures, by understanding our faults, judged not against another's standards, but against our own, best standards. In this exercise of self-examination we hope to gain a true perception of our own worth. This may at first humiliate us, but when the shame and embarrassment and annoyance fade, as it must if we have understood, it will lead to humility.

Or rather it will, if we also learn the second virtue it has to teach us – tolerance. Tolerance is not indifference, but we often think it so. There is a fear that to tolerate the faults of others, and perhaps even more so one's own, is to suggest that they do not matter. 'Even if God will forgive me,' we may say to ourselves, 'I never will. What I did was intolerable and unforgivable, and to suggest otherwise is to lessen the sin.' We sometimes have the feeling that to tolerate our own failings would be to let go of the whole intellectual or moral structure of our life; to tolerate failure is to undermine any subsequent chances of success.

It is possible to be intolerant and strict with the sin, and also tolerant and compassionate with the sinner, but it is difficult. Hence the value of the mundane realism of self-examination, because then we understand our own failings (and by extension those of others) not as the products of viciousness, but of quite ordinary, common failure, not so much separate acts as aspects of our character.

Where is the origin of our sin? The Bible is perhaps more instructive than we allow it to be. The biblical phrase 'the sin of Adam' is usually taken in a general sense to mean the sin of Adam *and* Eve, of men and women; but, sometimes, it may also mean more precisely Adam's sin rather than Eve's. This does make a difference, for it is widely assumed that Genesis 3, the story of the Fall, tells us that Eve was the first sinner, that it was the woman's fault. This is not so.

It was Eve who took the apple and ate. But was that a sin?

It did not contravene a prohibition, for we read earlier that God commanded Adam: 'But of the tree of knowledge of good and evil, *thou* shalt not eat of it' (Genesis 2.17). The command was given to Adam (in the second person singular), and not to Eve, for she had not yet been created (Genesis 2.22). It is true that in her desire to identify with her husband she exaggerates the extent of the command given to him alone (Genesis 3.3), but this is rather a quality than a fault; she is portrayed, as one American put it, 'as a real neat lady'. As she stood before the tree, it says of her, 'the woman saw that the tree was good for food, and that it was a delight to the eye, and desirable to make one wise' (Genesis 3.6). She makes a practical judgement, an aesthetic judgement and an intellectual judgement, in marked contrast to Adam, who (like a bureaucrat?) has instead spent his time giving names to all the animals.

The moment of sin is in Adam's reply to God's question, 'Hast thou eaten of the tree, of which I commanded thee that *thou* shouldest not eat?' (Genesis 3.11). We can almost guess the type of answer he will give, for, as he has just said, 'I was afraid'; but what an abject reply it is: 'The woman whom *thou* gavest to be with me, *she* gave me of the tree, and I ate' (Genesis 3.12). He blames God for giving him Eve, and then he blames her for giving him the fruit. His act of disobedience would not have gone unpunished, but this loss of integrity, this miserable failure to accept responsibility, this is more than just an act, it is sin.

'Incontinence' is the traditional term for such sin – an embarrassingly appropriate word. And like a sickness it is contagious, insinuating itself into our nature; when Eve is asked (note that there is no mention of a command disobeyed) she in turn blames the serpent (Genesis 3.13). While she might have stood her ground and insisted on her own freedom of action, she like Adam has allowed shame to grow and turns the accusation on to another. There we have it, the Original Sin in which we are all implicated – not the grand rebellion of a fallen angel, but the incontinence of a wimp.

This is by no means the complete description of a very rich and profound text, but it is valuable in order to correct the common misunderstanding, and to underline the shameful wretchedness of the sin portrayed. Not defiance, not even entirely disobedience, but mere abject weakness. It also provides a very clear contrast to the darker portrayal of sin in the next chapter of Genesis, in which Cain, for no reason, kills his brother Abel. There in Genesis 4 is the demon of sin, the horrifying evil of male violence. Yet even here the picture is not as simple as we may suppose, for Cain the murderer was the founder of the first city, and the grandsons of murder were the authors of civilization (Genesis 4.18–22).

Violence and incontinence, the two great poles of human sin, are described in these two chapters. The self-examination of study is concerned with the latter, and its value derives from the fact that we more naturally tend to think of sin under the first category, the act, rather than the second, the failure to act.

Violence and incontinence, the two poles of sin; the seven deadly sins; sins of commission and omission; mortal and venial sins; there are many ways of analysing and categorizing it, but they do not tell the whole story. Sin does not only mean the sum total of distinguishable sins, it is also part of the human condition, hidden from ourselves, so that it is impossible to effect a complete self-examination; we cannot uncover all our sin. As persons we are not whole and complete, and it is this that limits our self-knowledge.

There is a common debate between Free Will and Determinism. Either one or the other describes human behaviour; either we have a free will or our actions are determined. It arose in the eighteenth century as a product of the mechanistic view of science initiated by the Newtonian revolution. According to the Christian tradition, the dichotomy is illusory (or if you prefer, simplistic nonsense), and the philosophical conclusions derived from both sides of the debate are equally irrelevant.

We have a will, and this is possible because the world is ordered and determined and follows the laws of nature; chaos would be no context for human autonomy and consciousness. We have a will, but that will is not free: this is the problem of sin and the pain of the human condition that is ignored in the secular debate. Our will may be *constrained* by the limits of nature (we could not fly like a bird if we wanted to), but this is trivial next to the more important fact that our will is also *bound*.

If our wills were free, we should be whole and complete as persons and our actions would be consistent; but they aren't, and so we find the inner separation and struggle that Paul so graphically alludes to: 'I am a creature of flesh and blood, but sold as a slave to sin. I do not understand my own behaviour; I do not act as I intend to, but I do things I hate . . . . Though the will to do what is good is in me, the power to do it is not: the good I want to do, I never do; the evil that I do not want – that is what I do' (Romans 7.14–19). You and I neither have a *free* will nor are our actions predetermined: we have a will and, in Paul's phrase, it is a prisoner. That is why it is so hard, and ultimately impossible, to know ourselves fully.

How do we escape this terrible confusion? The full answer is found in Paul's proclamation of the gospel of salvation in the following chapter of Romans, but in the more modest context of this book, we would do well to remember a truth I have mentioned before – that our life is a pilgrimage. It is in moving and making progress that we learn.

We learn by our mistakes. This means that if we made no mistakes, we should learn nothing. This in turn means that condemnation, and the pointing out of our mistakes, is an important gift, to be warmly welcomed. It is a hard lesson, for none of us likes to be told off, criticized or condemned. In theory, and this is what we would like to believe, we could, with a clear head and a good heart, learn to behave well towards other people by our own efforts; in practice, we learn by the criticism of others, gentle, angry or tearful.

The Old Testament prophets are the clearest example of this truth, that condemnation is good for us. Take Amos the earliest of the written prophets: a later editor has softened his words a little and added a conclusion of hope, but the bulk of his proclamation is relentlessly and unmitigatingly harsh, 'all darkness, not light – pitch-black without a ray of brightness' (Amos 5.20). No wonder they didn't want his preaching at Bethel and suggested he return to his own home (Amos 7.10–13).

Later prophets were every bit as harsh in their condemnation of God's people – all of them speaking in God's name, a God whom we know loves us. We may be tempted to think that they would have been more effective as preachers if they had used a bit more encouragement or persuasion, a glimmer of hope and more positive teaching, instead of this unrelenting condemnation. But the great truth of their writing is that it was the condemnation of what was wrong that taught Israel the practice of what was right. It was Hosea's condemnation of the people's adultery that taught them the meaning of the love of God; it was Isaiah and others' accusations of forsaking the Law that taught the people the meaning of that Law. Or, as Paul put it with slightly different emphasis, sin preceded the law.

We fail and are condemned, and so learn what it is we should do, and as we learn, we fail again, and so on. It is a pilgrimage and we cannot stand still. It does not ease the pain and hurt of being condemned, but we can understand its value, to know that God's condemnation is for our good and one of his gifts. After all, if all he wanted to do was destroy us, he'd destroy us and that would be the end of it. If this Old Testament model sounds too harsh a mechanism of learning, consider how often Jesus himself introduces some of his most profound teaching to his disciples by first condemning them for their blindness or their lack of faith or their stupidity.

Is stupidity a sin? There are any number of vices, selfishness, arrogance, greed, envy and so on, that we would immediately understand as sinful, but is stupidity one of them? How often is a child reprimanded with the words, 'That was a stupid thing to do!', and then shamed and punished for that stupidity? I give one example from my own childhood. I possessed one of those little salt and pepper shakers, and carried it around proudly in my pocket. In the school playground I saw a friend lying on the ground looking up at the sky. I knew that pepper made one sneeze, so it seemed a good joke to sprinkle some over his face. He screamed with pain as it went into his eyes. While he was led off to have them seen to, I was roundly berated in a condemnation that centered on the words 'stupid' and 'idiot'. 'I didn't realize,' I pleaded, quite honestly. 'Well, you *should* have done,' I was told.

The misdeed was viciously cruel; all I had intended was a mild prank, to make him sneeze, and it never occurred to me that pepper could hurt the eyes, but that did not absolve me of the anger and the punishment. It was a sin, a sin of stupidity. We may not know a fact, and we may not have thought about the consequences of an action, but as a matter of conduct, behaviour and morality, we *should* have done.

The more you think about it, the more you can see faults, mistakes and misdeeds as being the result of stupidity; not malice but folly. Most of us have good intentions towards other people, so why do we hurt them so often? I do not intend to be a cold-hearted husband, an inconsiderate host or an insensitive visitor, but I am often too stupid to get it right.

All this is reasonably obvious, but we can pursue the idea further. Just exactly how intelligent are you? How much of your stupidity and ignorance is curable? Are you certain you could not be more intelligent than you are? We may talk about intelligence as though it were a separate faculty, but we know this is not true. There is not one part of our heart and brain exclusively concerned with intelligence (and stupidity) and another with being good (or bad); they may be distinguishable, but not separable.

If intelligence and its execution is not an isolated capacity, but part of our selves, then maybe your lack of intelligence is a question of character, and maybe your character is hindered and thwarted by your lack of intelligence. Now of course it would be arrogant as well as foolish to suppose that we could all be an Einstein or a Mother Teresa; genius is as much given by the grace of God as saintliness.

The question is not comparative, 'Could I be more intelligent than So-and-so?', nor is it an abstract absolute, 'Is there a limit to intelligence?'; it is entirely personal, 'Where is the limit to my intelligence?'

It seems that we could do just a bit better, find a bit more understanding; not simply try harder, but achieve more. We may call the limit one of intelligence, but it may equally be one of character and willpower. Never once in all my studies could I have proved, even to myself, that it was not a weakness or laziness of character that stopped me short. There remains the humbling and tantalizing suggestion that I have never quite touched the edge, the boundary of my intellect, beyond which I can go no further. It does not follow that I could get better and better indefinitely; there may be an edge, but I do not believe I have ever reached it.

What are the implications of this? First, that stupidity, which is the cause of much sin, may be the result of an inadequate application of one's intelligence, which itself may be the result of the more recognizable sins that we have been considering, impatience, laziness and so on. Precisely because stupidity can be so dangerous, it ought to be regarded and treated, at least in part, as a sin – so long, that is, as it is not based on comparisons with others (which of course, if you remember your school-days, it so often is).

Second, if intelligence is not confined, then how much less so is wisdom. I may never, realistically, become more intelligent, in the sense of gaining real mathematical competence or a deeper understanding of nuclear physics, but there is nothing to stop me becoming wiser. Wisdom is not measured out in relation to our innate intelligence, but it does come in proportion to how we *use* our intelligence.

When I wrote the first draft of Chapter 2 for a seminar, it was entitled 'Confessing One's Sins'; when I revised it as a chapter of this book it became 'Acquiring Self-knowledge'; I offer a final reflection on the connection between these two ideas.

When we reflect on our own actions, we tend to concentrate upon the intentions behind them; when we reflect upon the actions of others, we tend to see most clearly their results. In our own actions we stress the cause; in other people's, the effect. Unfortunately, as St Paul sadly stated, what we want and what we intend is not always the same as what we do and what occurs.

Such a disjunction between our self-perception and the perception of others would not be so serious, were it not for the other tendency to suppose, consciously or unconsciously, that our *self*-reflection is somehow privileged and superior to the judgement of others. It is evidently different, but is it closer to the truth?

It is the richness of our self-knowledge that is part of its compulsion: we know not only our public acts, but all the thoughts behind them, the hopes and fears and dreams, that seem so much more interesting than mere deeds. It is not just the odd secret but the whole wealth of the private world of the mind, with its huge collection of memories, its wide range of emotions and its swarming hive of plans.

Who knows you better? You or other people? By which I mean not '*an*other person', but 'other people in general' considered as an hypothetical whole, able to pool their partial, individual knowledge. There is perhaps a natural tendency to favour ourselves; we know ourselves best of all, other people in varying and lesser degrees, and God hardly at all. The Christian tradition may not have proposed the precise question, but it suggests a reverse order of knowledge. God knows us best of all (and this without having to peer into our innermost thoughts – an idea that used to scare me horribly as a child), other people as a whole know us well, and we ourselves often rather poorly.

We can all accept, because we have seen it in others, that it is possible to develop a grossly inflated and overly flattering self-image. It is not enough to say, '*I* wouldn't be like that'; we need a more solid corrective than our own good intentions. I can remember in almost exact detail the classroom and the occasion when a teacher shouted at me, 'You're so arrogant!' I didn't even know what the word meant. As I sat in the library staring at the dictionary definition, I gradually realized that someone, not even in my family, knew something about the inside of me, that I myself was not yet aware of. It was uncomfortably threatening, an assault into my own private world, but a valuable lesson.

I have said that we need to examine ourselves because others cannot do it for us. This is true for the details, but the initial clues come from them. If you are fortunate to have a piece of work judged and corrected by a teacher, it is those judgements from which you begin. Part of the exercise is to see yourself through the eyes of another, not simply because it is a different perspective, but because it is a better perspective.

It is inevitable that the condemnation of others may at times be motivated by envy and malice, or made worthless by ignorance, but such prosecution will not suffer from self-deception. The accusation of a friend may not be the voice of God, but it is probably closer to it than our own self-judgement.

To see ourselves as God sees us – that is true wisdom and understanding. To see our sins through his eyes would be quite simply to know everything about ourselves, and above all to *know* (and not merely to assent to the fact of) how much we are loved.

These reflections upon the character of sin may seem

either too extensive and too removed from the exercise of examining a product of study, or else too inadequate for so vast a topic. All I have intended is to show how broad a realm of self-knowledge can be opened out by so simple a task.

If therefore you have the opportunity to see your writing in print, or your picture framed, or your cooking placed before a formal, public gathering, seek to examine it from a distance, as though it were the work of another. Assume the sensitivity and courtesy you would for a friend or a colleague, and then apply a thorough criticism. Try to understand both what is being achieved, and the failure to achieve it.

What makes the effort worthwhile is that it is genuinely possible (and without self-deception) to move quite beyond the feelings of shame and remorse, to move beyond as it were the condemnation of sin, and to see one's work and what it means and the person who did it as something of real interest and fascination – and that includes the failings and limitations. Especially if you are a person of low self-esteem, it can be one of the most effective means of seeing yourself as others do, of grasping your true self-worth.

Chapter 8

Getting Ready for Judgement

If life were like school, how would our performance be judged, by continuous assessment or by exam? 'Life isn't fair' may be one of a grandmother's earliest pieces of wisdom to a bewildered and complaining grandchild, and it is the exam which prevails in life, however unfair that may seem, not continuous assessment, as we saw in Chapter 3. We also find the exam model not just within life but for our life itself, for we do not know what the Last Judgement will be like, and we cannot know how God will judge us. As with all else about the after-life, we cannot have knowledge in this world.

What we can have, based on faith, revelation and reason, is a coherent model for this future event, an idea that makes sense and that can guide our lives in the best way possible. The idea of continuous assessment suggests that God will weigh all the good that we do against all the evil, his judgement depending on which is the heavier. For most people this seems the more attractive notion, for we are generally optimists in our own regard, and it would appear probable that the end result will be in our favour.

There are however two dangers. If we lead an ordinary life, governed by good intentions, we shall be prone to complacency. If the verdict is by the sum total of our behaviour, then it follows that no single act, or failure to act, is of itself decisive. No single thing that we do matters that much, for it is only part of a greater whole. If we fail today, there is always tomorrow to make amends, or the good marks of yesterday to fall back on; today is not ultimately important.

Suppose however that you have led an inordinately wicked life, caught up in drug smuggling, in the army of a totalitarian regime, or in a mafia clan. If at last, after years of sin, you repent and change your ways, is there any future for you but despair? Is not the balance of evil so great that the whole of the rest of your life can never hope to redress it? A view of life that leads either to despair or to complacency is surely a wrong one.

The Christian tradition has, however, stressed the approach to life as an exam, with death and the Last Judgement as *the* exam. Such an idea has of course waned, for in time of peace, good hospitals and greater longevity, the prospects of a sudden or early death are very much less than they were. Nevertheless it is the only notion of judgement that holds out any hope.

Ezekiel 18 is the first great text on this subject. Whole books have been written just on this chapter, so I shall not attempt more than a swift glance; it is often entitled 'Individual Responsibility', but it goes further than that. Ezekiel preached to the scattered people of Judah, exiled in Babylon after the fall of Jerusalem, a people weighed down by the burden of past sins, in despair because the former sins of the nation were more than they could ever remedy. They quoted the cynical proverb: 'The parents have eaten unripe grapes and the children's teeth are set on edge' (Ezekiel 18.2). Ezekiel vehemently rejects the idea that the weight of sin can be passed down from one generation to the next, until it builds up to such an extent that all is apathy and hopelessness: 'The one who has sinned is the one who must die; a son is not to bear his father's guilt, nor a father his son's guilt' (Ezekiel 18.20).

What the Lord has taught Ezekiel, and what he is teaching the exiled, is that the sins of the past cannot set the agenda for the future. It is the present, a present that leads into the future, that matters. Not only is an individual not to be tied to the past sins of a former generation, neither is he to be tied to his own past sins. 'If the wicked man, however, renounces all the sins he has committed, respects my laws and is law-abiding and upright, he will most certainly live; he will not die . . . I do not take pleasure in the death of a wicked man, but rather that he should turn from his wickedness and live' (Ezekiel 18.21, 23). If we are to live our lives effectively, it is the present that concerns us, and if we are to avoid complacency and despair there must be a future that unfolds for us, a future that we can do something about, for which we can prepare. This is the main insight of Ezekiel's revelation.

We do not know the future; therefore we have to act now, to take risks and to commit our selves and our life. Wise and gentle encouragement is given by the writer of Ecclesiastes:

> Cast your bread upon the waters,
> for after many days you will find it again.
> Give portions to seven, even to eight,
> for you do not know what disaster
> may fall upon the land. (Ecclesiastes 11.1–2)

You do not know what may go wrong, so do not put all your eggs into one basket; rather be generous in your work and your enterprises, so that if some fail, there will remain others to succeed.

We have to work harder, in study, prayer or life, if we cannot tell beforehand what will be needed:

> Sow your seed in the morning,
> and in the evening let not your hands be idle,
> for you do not know which will succeed,
> whether this or that,
> or whether both will do equally well. (Ecclesiastes 11.6)

Risk and wastage cannot be avoided in our lives, therefore sow your seed generously, that you may be assured of a harvest. Always prepare more than enough, just in case.

Can one cheat? By definition, we cannot cheat God, but is there something in the exam model that allows it to be a cunning short cut to salvation? This is unlikely if its principal exhortation is to do *more* study, prayer or work, than one is inclined to do. Certainly at university, which is my only experience, I have found (not surprisingly) that this model of preparing for an exam is the best form of teaching for students preparing for an exam. Life itself is far more complicated and far more unpredictable, so that the model should be yet more successful.

I was, however, proved wrong by one student. He was especially cunning and was in no way going to cast his bread upon the waters. He studied the regulations and past exam papers and worked out exactly what was the minimum needed for success: he took the narrowest possible syllabus and applied himself to that alone, rejecting anything that did not fall within that compass. He gained First Class Honours.

What can be said in mitigation? He was extremely clever, and his plan never worked when taken up by lazier or less intelligent students. But more importantly, he was ambitious and a First was only a means to a higher end: he knew what he wanted and he went for it. Whether he was as innocent as a dove I don't know, but he was certainly as cunning as a serpent, and as such would have been commended by Jesus. His was not a lazy option, but a single-minded one – he *knew* his crisis and he had prepared for it.

Most of us, most of the time, do not know, and it is on this basis that the model holds true. Build up a wealth of wisdom, knowledge, goodness, and prayer, and we will not be taken by surprise; keep your wardrobe to a minimum and you may be caught without a wedding garment. As Jesus himself said: 'The good man draws what is good from the store of goodness in his heart; the evil man draws what is evil from the store of evil. For from the overflow of the heart come the words of the mouth' (Luke 6.45). It is a *store* of goodness we seek, full to overflowing.

What is our Lord's teaching on the subject? It is contained in Matthew 25.31–46, and known as the Parable of the Sheep and the Goats. It is rather more than just a parable for it presents a vision of the Last Judgement, but it is clear that it is not a propositional statement. This may seem obvious, but it is important to remember, for it is too often seen as a problem text, in that it seems to deny the gospel of grace, by substituting salvation by good works.

Jesus is, however, giving not a measured statement of doctrine, but an arresting passage of teaching, not to the world in general but to Christians, to his disciples. It is the final passage of the teaching of Jesus, as Matthew has presented it; immediately after it begins the narrative of the Passion. Looking forward to the end of all things, the Lord instructs his followers how to prepare for the Last Judgement.

If this chapter is shorter than others, it is because I want to lay all the emphasis on this central passage in the teaching of Jesus:

> When the Son of Man comes in his glory, and all the angels with him, then will he sit on his throne of glory. All nations will be gathered before him, and he will separate the people one from another as a shepherd separates the sheep from the goats; and he will place the sheep on his right hand, but the goats on the left.
>
> Then the King will say to those on his right hand, 'Come, you who are blessed of my Father, inherit the kingdom prepared for you from the foundation of the world. For I was hungry, and you gave me food; I was thirsty, and you gave me drink; I was a stranger, and you took me in; I was naked, and you clothed me; I was sick, and you visited me; I was in prison, and you came to me.'
>
> Then the righteous will answer him, 'Lord, when did we see you hungry and feed you, or thirsty and give you drink? When did we see you a stranger and take you in, or naked and clothe you? When did we see you sick or in prison and come to you?'
>
> And the King will answer them, 'In truth I tell you, inasmuch as you did this to one of the least of my brothers, you did it to me.'
>
> Then he will say to those on his left, 'Depart from me,

you cursed, into the eternal fire prepared for the devil and his angels. For I was hungry and you gave me no food; I was thirsty and you gave me no drink; I was a stranger and you did not take me in; naked and you did not clothe me; sick and in prison and you did not visit me.'

Then they also will answer, 'Lord, when did we see you hungry or thirsty or naked or sick or in prison, and did not minister to you?'

Then he will answer them, 'In truth I tell you, inasmuch as you did not do this to one of the least of these, you did not do it to me.' And they will go away to eternal punishment, but the righteous to eternal life.

The parable is well known and much loved, but in my experience its striking lesson is usually missed. Perhaps Christians are too philosophical, too ready to assume a comprehensive picture of the world, so that this parable has been seen as a rounded and balanced summary, rather than an arresting exclamation mark, a final shock to our complacency.

The image is taken from that of a shepherd in Palestine who tends his sheep and goats together on the hillside during the day, and now separates them at night; goats, so the commentaries tell us, need to be kept warm, while the sheep with thicker fleeces can fend for themselves in the cold. Whatever the reason, it is worth noting that the sheep and the goats of the Near East are remarkably similar to look at, unlike their European counterparts; the main way of telling them apart is that goats' short tails stick up, sheep's long tails hang down. It is a pastoral image developed into a grand tableau of a king before all the peoples of the world. As the final item of Jesus's teaching ministry it is clearly a very important text.

Before we consider the parable itself, it is helpful to consider its context and look at the two preceding parables. The first (Matthew 25.1–13) is about the Wise and Foolish Virgins, ten of whom took extra oil for their lamps and so were ready when the bridegroom came at midnight, ten of whom came unprepared and so their lamps went out. Although they immediately went to get more oil, they found the doors closed against them when they returned. 'Stay awake, therefore, because you do not know the day or the hour' (Matthew 25.13).

This is followed by the parable of the Talents (Matthew 25. 14–30), in which the master gives his three servants five, two and one talent each before going away for a long time. On his return, he praises the two servants who have increased the treasure he gave them, and roundly condemns the one who has added nothing. 'Take the talent from him, and give it to the man who has ten. For everyone who has will be given more, and he will have an abundance; but anyone who has not, even what he has will be taken from him' (Matthew 25.28–9). Add to your store of talents and you will receive still more; do nothing, believing (or hoping) you have enough, and even that will be taken from you, at the final testing.

The coming of the Bridegroom, the return of the Master, and now finally the last judgement of the King. To the sheep he says, 'Come, you blessed of my Father . . . for I was hungry and you gave me food, I was thirsty and you gave me drink . . .' (Matthew 25.34–5). Not surprisingly, they are unaware of ever having helped their King, and they reply, 'Lord, when did we see you hungry and feed you, or thirsty and give you to drink . . . ?' (Matthew 25.37). The King says to them, 'In truth I tell you, inasmuch as you did this to one of the least of my brothers, you did it to me' (Matthew 25.40). While to the goats, after a similar exchange, but coming to the opposite conclusion, he replies, 'In truth I tell you, inasmuch as you did not do this to one of the least of these, you did not do it to me' (Matthew 25.45). This clearly is the heart of the parable. What does it mean?

Bible translation is no easy task, but if there were a prize for the silliest translation of all, it should perhaps go to the Good News Bible for its version of these two verses: 'The King will reply, 'I tell you, whenever you did this for one of the least important of these brothers of mine, you did it for me!' (Matthew 25.40). 'Whenever'. Taken that most of us do not lead lives that are wholly good or wholly bad, but a mixture of the two, it follows that we are by turns both sheep and goats; whenever we do something good, we are among the sheep, and whenever we do something bad, we are among the goats, so presumably both the reward and the punishment will come to each one of us. This makes the central image of the division between the two nonsense, and Jesus as teacher something of a fool.

If we accept that this passage is Christ's teaching, and that his teaching is vivid and true, there must be an understanding of these two crucial verses that makes sense of the parable as a whole, that is consistent with the rest of his teaching, remembering that it is a story urging us to be ready for final judgement.

The key word is 'one'. It is usually taken to mean 'anyone', as in 'inasmuch as you did it to anyone of the least of my brothers', but again this weakens the meaning of the parable. If anyone, or everyone, of my brothers and sisters is Christ, it does not greatly matter whether I help that person when they knock on my door today, because I can always help them (perhaps more effectively) tomorrow; we return to the sterile notion of a balance between all our good deeds and all our bad. If everyone is Christ, is that any different to nobody being Christ?

It is generally the case in Jesus's parables that the punchline is surprising and striking, forcing us to rethink our assumptions. So then, what if 'one' here really does mean one and not more – 'just one' or '*the* one'? That of all the people throughout our life who are in need of our help, just one of them is for us Christ himself. That thought concentrates the mind!

Most of the Lord's brothers and sisters are for us no more and no less than that; but for you, in your life, *one*, just one of them, is Jesus himself. You will not know who he is or when he will come or what he will ask, all you can know is that he or she will come at a time you least expect, perhaps even when you are worn out and exhausted, and all but unable to help anyone. Now this is a powerful idea.

There is no continual assessment here, but the one single crisis when we come face to face with our Lord, the one moment that will focus our entire life. Either our faith is real, we have followed Christ's command to love one another, and we are obedient to our duty to his brothers and sisters, in which case we shall be prepared and will pass the test, and be counted among the blessed, or our faith and love and duty are not real, and we will not pass the test, and will be cast out to eternal punishment.

If you received an invitation to the palace it would be easy, you could put away your evil deeds, buy new clothes and be ready to meet your King; but if he is disguised as one of his subjects, then are you not obliged to treat all of them with due respect and generosity, if you do not wish to be rejected by him? He will seek you out and you can be sure you will not know him; or why else would he be in disguise?

As Jesus himself said, 'You may be quite certain of this, that if the householder had known at what hour of the night the burglar was going to come, he would have stayed awake and not let his house be broken into' (Matthew 24.43). There is absolutely nothing you can do to discover when and where the Son of Man will come to you: that meeting is unknown and unknowable; therefore stay awake.

Jesus did not invent the Parable of the Sheep and the Goats to torment us, but to underline a most important truth about the world as it is. Crises do happen; but we can learn to prepare for them. Our judgement will come; but we can learn to be ready.

Chapter 9

Living within Limits

Study is a privilege, even if it never seemed so at school. Not so much for the provision and the quality of the teaching, as the opportunity itself and the time required. To have the time to study – this is the privilege. I have been very conscious when writing this book of the many people who do not have this privilege of time, that is to say anyone for whom life itself is a struggle, whether it is in searching for the next meal, or a job, or a solution to family problems.

There is both a quantity and a quality of time needed, a physical and mental freedom from other concerns, that makes study a privilege, in the sense that it cannot be guaranteed to all. If this privilege comes, therefore, we must use it to the full, in the pursuit of wisdom and for the sake of others. Does that sound pompous? Perhaps it is better to put the argument the other way round: that the opportunity for study is a privilege is not the reason to reject it, nor to pretend it is only for other people.

And prayer? To learn and practise prayer, beyond a simple supplication to God, does demand a quantity and a quality of time; yet prayer is not seen as a privilege, nor is it exclusively for those with leisure. So too I believe with the pattern of study I have been analysing. What is certain is that most people have more time for it than they will admit. 'I'm too tired' or 'I can't be bothered' are justifiable excuses after a day's work sometimes, but not always. Mental fitness like physical fitness needs discipline, and that is rarely possible unless it becomes a habit.

There are two principal obstacles to using what time we

have available for the discipline of study and prayer – effort and wastage. Effort is the obvious one, and I have alluded to the difficulty many times; however often we tell ourselves it won't be so bad once we begin, the lethargy remains and with it the temptation to do nothing. The realization that much of our effort, if applied, will be wasted is a more subtle disincentive. What you work at today may never be useful, may never be needed, or may never come to fruition, but at least (unlike physical exercise perhaps) it will never be lost – even forgetting something again and again is not the same as never having known it.

Both are quite unavoidable and only the fostering of a habit is proof against them. However, unlike such skills as those of sport or computing, wisdom is available for a life-time and is not dependent on physical or mental abilities. I know I shall not become wise in a decade, but perhaps, I say to myself, around the age of seventy, I might be. No doubt then I will change the time-scale to when I am eighty, but no matter.

One thing is certain, it takes time to become wise. While many of the elderly are by no means wise, some truly are, and it is an extraordinary grace. One of my great heroes in this respect was Michael Ramsey, 100th Archbishop of Canterbury and one of the great Christian leaders of this century; in that position he was certainly a great man, but I was mostly too young to notice. But after he retired and left behind the cares of office, he gained a still greater quality of wisdom that was awesome, and inspired all who met him, however briefly. It is a beautiful grace that still flowers so late.

I developed this discipline of study as prayer in part because I did not have the time, the quality of unworried time, for too much pure prayer. Yet now I find the main encouragement in the fact that there is so much time, or at least no time limit other than death. It is possible because it is a long-term undertaking, stretching open-ended for the rest of one's life.

It is important therefore to study with this sense of time always in mind. If there happens to be a deadline in the form of an exam or an appraisal, that is only temporary. I have to finish a painting or cook a meal by a certain time, but there is the next one, and the next. One does not so much start again, as continue where one left off.

Time itself is part of the process. I do not know what my mind is up to when I am not looking at it, but it does not go to sleep. Take part in a discussion, worry a subject to death, work out the definitive conclusion or think yourself to a standstill, but then put it away or forget about it, and when you return a few days, weeks, months or even years later, your thoughts have moved on: time has worked on your mind, even if you were never conscious of it.

The word needs, in Cranmer's phrase, to be inwardly digested. How? In large part, and this is the encouraging bit, by doing nothing. All the same, our time though long is not infinite. It is finite and so are we: we have to draw a conclusion before our time is up and every loose end drawn in; thus all we do is imperfect. To know that fact and to be able to use that understanding does make an important difference. As I tried to show in Chapter 4, it offers a particular direction to what we seek to achieve.

A simple example came to me as I sat down to write this chapter. Someone called and asked for help in writing a funeral telegram. These are very important features of our island funerals, when families may be scattered hundreds if not thousands of miles around the Atlantic, with no transport available for anything up to a month. Somehow in a few words sons and daughters have to give thanks and offer prayers for the life of someone they have loved, to be read out at the distant service the next day. Some families try to make it perfect, to say everything, and the result is a list of superlatives that has lost any meaning and could apply to anyone or no one. Some are too scared to try, and the telegram speaks of the mourners and not the person who has died. But some know the impossibility of saying it all and yet the need to say something, and the results can be very striking and moving – inadequate, imperfect, and exactly right.

If I seem to insist too much on imperfection, it is because I want to show that it is not merely inevitable but necessary, and not only necessary but useful as a guiding principle. It is also because every area of study is guided by the experts, the most brilliant and the most knowledgeable: they themselves may not claim to be perfect or their work complete, but to most students they appear so far ahead it may seem hard to suppose otherwise. The certainty that everyone is fallible is not of itself enough to encourage the beginner to criticize the master. More than that, study itself, however you view it, appears to be for the clever; the rules, the norms, the exercises are devised by and for those who are clever.

Of course we want to be taught by those who know the subject best, not by those who know it least; but this does not alter the fact that we ourselves can feel too overawed to follow. There are some students who never dare to move forward or commit themselves to a judgement, for fear of not being good enough, being shown up for their stupidity, or being shamed for their slowness – people who having read one introduction to the subject will then read another, and then another, who if it comes to a discussion always seek to stay or to return to square one.

The little slogan I drew out for myself and pasted to the wall by my desk at university simply said 'Stop Reading!' Lazy students, myself included, often have a natural affinity for the book subjects, in which there is a vast amount of reading matter, rather than the sparser subjects, such as languages or mathematics. You cannot read much about French, you can only learn it, and that is hard work, whereas in history, there is so much written on any one period, you need never run out of new material.

On the face of it, the poor student with no academic self-confidence may find the sheer number of books overwhelming, but at the same time, perhaps unconsciously, strangely comforting – there is enough here in which to lose oneself. It seems studious to spend hour after hour devouring book after book, marking page after page of notes, and the intention appears worthy, for there is always more information to be gathered, other viewpoints to be considered, other experts to be consulted.

The student would plead, 'I want to read another book, because I do not yet understand the subject; and you told me not to rush ahead in impatience.' It sounds convincing, but it is important to remember that a book is rarely the subject of study itself, it is about the subject, and only points towards the particular theme, idea or concept; it is this which one is called to study. At some point, you must stop reading and go beyond what you have read.

An aside. When you were reading, say, Chapters 1 and 2 of this little book, did you stop and put those two exercises into practice? Did you put aside the book for a few days and get down to the hard work it suggested? The chances are that you didn't, for it is easier and less demanding to carry on reading.

Study is hard work. As the popular joke goes, 'Work, I love it: I can watch it for hours.' Reading a book or listening to someone talk is, too often, not work, but watching someone else work.

The importance of the notion of imperfection is that it is not a statement about where you are now, for this is readily admissible, but about the goal you aim at. You are not seeking perfection: therefore you cannot use your own inadequacy and imperfection as an excuse for not venturing forward, into the difficult realm of thinking, speaking or writing for yourself.

Within all areas of study and prayer we do *not* seek perfection, but the best that is possible within the prevailing constraints.

The most productive constraints are those which we cannot choose ourselves. This is the extraordinary merit of what I earlier described as 'crisis', when a specific problem is set before us or a quite specific question is asked – a limited task within a limiting context. Any notion of giving a perfect answer simply does not arise: it is not everything that is being asked for, but something quite definite.

One of the perennial frustrations for all clergy is the common request or desire, always from the most occasional church-goers, for the 'perfect sermon'; one has to keep reminding oneself that it is not merely one's own inadequacy that fails to produce one, it is an unrealizable dream for any preacher. The sermon is designed for the quite limited task of answering the specific questions that arise from the reading of the Word of God and the life of the congregation. A simple rhetorical presentation of God, the Universe and Everything is an absurdity.

If this sounds like special pleading, look more closely at the Bible itself. Jesus's teaching is remarkably constrained: here is no holy man sitting on a mountain pouring out generalized, universal truths; his parables are in answer to actual questions or immediate complaints; they have a precise context, with the constraints this imposes. Even the Sermon on the Mount, which is the most deliberately general collection of Christ's teaching, has in fact surprisingly few universal commands and exhortations, and many more specific ones which together build up a picture broader than themselves.

St Paul's letters to the young churches are a yet clearer example of how narrow is the compass of so much of Scripture – the immediate concerns of particular people and communities. Romans is the least limited by a context, but nevertheless remains a letter to a particular church at a particular time. As are the words of the Old Testament prophets, with the possible exception of some of their oracles against the nations, which also happen to be generally the least valuable parts of their preaching.

When however the constraints are not imposed by outside

circumstances, but have to be decided, it is no easy task to know which are appropriate. It is easier to watch others suffer from a lack of constraint. My own recent example was the local computer club, formed to discuss and swap ideas on the latest advances in hard- and software. I was constantly assured that such and such a package *could* do just about everything, but I left after a few weeks because I was unable to find anyone who had actually *done* anything; it seemed as though the greater the possibilities, the fewer the results.

Why is mixed media art so rarely of value? To combine the best effects of different media should produce something better than any one on its own, but it doesn't. Why is so little good music produced by modern computer synthesizers? This single instrument can produce the sounds of twenty, and yet it never matches even one of the originals. And then again, I often wonder, as someone with a very modest IQ, why those in the 'genius' level and beyond so rarely achieve what one might expect from them.

If you have ever played made-up games in a school playground, you will know how much effort and enjoyment can go into the devising and modifying of rules. But in most activities it is not a matter of choice, but of judgement, according to one's perceptions of the situation. To invent constraints is unproductive; to decide which are appropriate, if none appear imposed, is however frustratingly difficult.

What example do we have to guide us? One that does not appear to offer any practical advice, but remains a guiding principle all the same: the incarnation of the Word of God, the deliberate self-limiting of God, to come to us as a man, so that we might see and know his love. It is not just the fact that Jesus Christ was born, but the whole truth of his incarnation, the *form* of his life and teaching and passion.

We may never be perfect, but can we ever be original? If it is the Truth that we seek, however modestly, then our task is to search for it, wait for it, even struggle with it, but surely not invent it. If Truth is somehow *there* (I keep the terms deliberately vague), it is for us to discover it. This does not present problems to a Christian who believes in God and in his Truth, but it does seem to back us into a corner, suggesting an attitude of quietism, of humble obedience and passive submission.

One cannot lightly dismiss notions of self-expression or self-fulfilment, or denigrate the romantic image of the impassioned artist, or suppress the desire to be different. But if we are asking a question as direct as 'Should one seek to be original in one's thinking, writing, painting, or whatever?', the answer has to be an emphatic 'No, never!', not because it is somehow wrong, but because it is self-defeating.

It is probably necessary to encourage new and young students to try to be original, otherwise there is the danger of their being crushed by the weight of existing scholarship. When you know full well that your own piece of work will never remotely approach the standard of the authorities you are required to consult, it can be hard to find any real purpose to it; you are defeated before you begin. To be shown how to break free from the weight of the past is an invaluable lesson.

The deliberate search for originality for its own sake may do wonders for a beginner's self-confidence, but as one matures within any subject, it becomes unnecessary and even a hindrance. The realization that there is a problem to be solved, an anomaly to be explained, or simply the feeling that there is more to be understood, should be enough to motivate further study and reflection.

If you come up with an answer, that is alone sufficient; whether it is original or not is neither here nor there. If you turn out to be a second Edison or Darwin, it will not be a desire for originality that does it. The desire is useful to get your elders and betters off your back; after that, it is best unlearned. It is an undisciplined desire, and can lead to the acceptance of a false idea, simply because it looks new.

Originality is not only self-defeating in such areas as

Greek translation but also in the freer, more expressive arts. I am not an artist, but I would still claim that the humble discipline of prayer would help one's art. As I said before, it makes no claim on the form of the art (it is not biased to realism), but it is a discipline that forces you to seek not *your* truth, but *the* truth. It is because this is the tougher discipline that it produces better results.

It is not originality that means anything; it is creativity. The Church has a prayer in the marriage service that begins: 'Heavenly Father, maker of all things, you enable us to share in your work of creation; bless this couple in the gift and care of children . . .' It is a pity that it seems to restrict this creativity to the more obvious gift of children, for in most of our life we are enabled to share in God's work. Any building up of order out of chaos, any development of a new perception or a cogent theory, any revelation of the truth is a share in the work of creation.

Establishing a family and building up its affections, habits and values is as much a share in the work of creation as giving birth to babies. In the same marriage service the couple promise 'to love and to cherish' each other. Why the need for this second verb? What sense does it carry, not fully expressed in the first? It underlines the action of love over time, the slow, creative, building of the relationship and the home, caring for, fostering, nurturing. Like tending or cultivating a young plant.

Indeed gardening is also, more modestly, a good example of creativity, for it is evident that the principal power is of God, and yet we are enabled to share in it, to offer our work and experience, without which the garden would not happen. All the books and expertise in the world will only help you so far; in the end it is up to you, for you are building or maintaining not gardens in general, but this garden here and now. Furthermore, it cannot be done in a hurry; you have to work with the seasons and imagine and plan for years to come.

This creativity, like wisdom itself, is a gift of God. Like every grace, it cannot be earned or grasped. To seek it too earnestly is therefore self-defeating. Wait for the truth, and you will be creative. Be creative, and you may be called 'original', but by then it will no longer matter.

'Great is truth, and it shall prevail' (1 Esdras 4.41). That curiously dull and uninspired work, known as 'Greek Ezra', was possibly numbered among the books of the Apocrypha solely on the strength of its description of the contest of the three young men before King Darius, in which each must state which single thing is the strongest, and justify that judgement. Zerubbabel wins by proclaiming that women are the strongest, but Truth is greater still; it orders the universe and endures for ever.

The philosophical details do not matter, but it is essential to hold a high view of Truth. We do not need a mystical vision nor a metaphysical theory, but we do need to understand that Truth carries its own authority and needs no further justification. Why? Not because it matters much what philosophy or theology we tentatively attempt to sketch out, but because we need a right view of ourselves.

We can never have the last word. We are only part of a broader pilgrimage, partners with our fellow travellers. Of course we may desire praise and recognition for our work, but we must not take ourselves too seriously. If Truth is great and it shall prevail, then we are its servants or its children, and never its master or creator. Ours is a humble task, and we should not be fooled by flattery.

What we should hope for is to share our small vision of the truth in such a way that it does not have our signature written upon it; like a window, we hope to pass on the light so that nothing is lost or distorted. Unfortunately, it is impossible, soiled as we are, to be invisible, but we can be superseded.

When I was teaching at college, newly ordained curates used to return from time to time to see old friends. Many would loudly insist, with a metaphorical sweep of the hand, that 'everything we were taught at college was useless – it's of no relevance in a parish!' This could of course have been a straightforward indictment of the teaching, but it could also have been its vindication. Had we in fact taught them sufficiently well that they were genuinely free and could now move beyond the teaching and on to the next stage of their maturing as deacons and priests?

If you are a spiritual director, or just a friend hoping to help, do you want the person who comes to you for counsel and advice to remain for ever under your influence, to become almost a disciple? No, of course not. If you have learned to listen, have acquired a deep knowledge of yourself, and have prepared for such an eventuality, you cannot but want to give all you have. If you have been privileged enough to help another gain freedom, from sorrow, guilt or fear, then you must want them to remain free. If you have managed to help others after a time of suffering, you want them to carry on growing, to outgrow *you*. This is real success, to be no longer needed, to be superseded.

It is a hard lesson to learn or to accept, because when someone no longer wants or needs you, is this because you have succeeded or because you have failed? Why can we never know? In the words of John Keble, 'God never lets us know the result of our actions. On the one hand, this keeps us hopeful and on the other, it keeps us humble.'

Chapter 10

The Next Step

In the Christian tradition, wisdom is the word and the spirit of God, the whole ordering of the universe. Wisdom (with a capital W) is the handmaid of the Lord in the Old Testament, the first-born of all creation (Proverbs 8.22). In the New Testament, wisdom becomes incarnate in Christ, whom Paul calls directly 'the Wisdom of God' (1 Corinthians 1.24). By the years of the early Fathers, Wisdom is a synonym for the Word of John 1, for the Second Person of the Trinity in relation to God's creation, for Christ as the one who orders the universe.

If I began this book by saying that wisdom is a gift of God, I end it by saying that wisdom is God. We seek, in the end, to share not merely a gift from God, but the nature of God himself. By wisdom we begin to perceive how we may come 'to share in the divinity of Christ, who humbled himself to share in our humanity'.

Such thoughts bring us into the great richness of Christian theology, to the tradition handed on for two thousand years. They need, like all truths, to be examined afresh and proclaimed again in our own generation, but that is beyond the scope of this book. I do not wish to justify the vision of wisdom on which I have relied, but rather like so many others, am content to say, 'Go to the Fathers, and they will teach you', or yet more directly, 'Go to Wisdom, the Son of God, and he will teach you.'

If such a conclusion is too grandiose and too generalized, let me reflect briefly on that key aspect of theology I alluded to in the last chapter. What does the incarnation mean – in practical terms – for our understanding of wisdom?

When we arrive in heaven, as I have said before, we shall no longer need wisdom for our knowledge will be complete. We shall all be wise, and none of us will need wisdom as a gift of grace. Perhaps also, here on earth, if we were immortal we could dispense with it, for we could allow knowledge and understanding to come by almost any means if time were limitless.

It is because we are mortal and finite that we need to apply ourselves to the path of wisdom, to seek understanding rather than simply wait for it to come. We as human beings seek the vision and knowledge of the divine. This is possible only because God himself became man. The incarnation of God cannot be restricted entirely to the life of Jesus of Nazareth; if it was true of the Son of God then, it is true of the Son of God now, or again, it is not so much that God *was* incarnate as that he *is* (always) incarnate.

The incarnation of God, the truth that the Divine can and does, by the mystery of the Trinity and in a manner beyond our grasp, come down and limit himself to the mortal human world, is the practical basis for our pursuit of wisdom. We are able to share God's wisdom, not because we reach up to him, but because he came down to us.

If we believe in incarnation as a fact about our world, it explains how it is possible to share the divine perception, how two realms, between which a great gulf has been fixed, can in truth meet. It means also that wisdom is not a form of mysticism; it is not seeking any esoteric knowledge beyond this world; if God is present in our world, this is scope enough. It also explains how our perception can move from the sublime to the ridiculous, from the universal to the particular; we are called to understand not only the stars but our nagging neighbour, to contemplate the mystery of life and to keep the house clean. 'Who sweeps a room as for thy laws' shares the vision of God, because God too lived in a room. And lastly, it suggests that if the wisdom of God has entered our universe through Christ, we would do well to reflect upon his word, his ministry and his passion.

Sooner or later, wisdom leads us to consider the great questions of love and suffering, of sin and reconciliation. The wise must at the last stand at the foot of the cross if they are to gain understanding and pierce the mystery. Here the ordering of the universe is laid bare, and both God and our selves most clearly revealed. Not that knowledge is easy here, but that this is the place where we shall find it. But this too is beyond the scope of this book.

It is probable, even reading slowly and even pausing a few days between each chapter, that the time taken to digest this book has been far shorter than the time needed to learn its techniques. It seems impertinent to suggest that you read the book a second time, though this may have the real advantage of taking the core ideas, which are not intended to be original, away from the author's particular bias and the limitations of his expression. One can only effectively use a skill that is one's own; while it remains borrowed from another, its usefulness is cramped and constrained.

I had planned, by way of conclusion, to summarize the four techniques and what one might hope to gain from them, but I realize this would have been counter-productive. If they were that simple, they would have been learned already, and to summarize them would be to harden them into a particular form, and so limit their further development.

Continue to follow the exercises, until they become a comfortable habit. Continue to reflect on their purpose until this too becomes plain and clear. After that, let the Spirit lead, and leave this book behind. The difficult period is between the first flush of enthusiasm and the moment when one can perceive a real advance. This could be as short as a few weeks; it was for me a matter of years.

The best advice I can give is first of all to follow such instructions as you can extract from this book and that you can fit into your present forms of study. When this begins to fail or your energy begins to flag, write up each exercise in your own words, with your own modifications, and according to how you intend to practise it.

At that point lay aside this book, and only some time later (I would say no less than six months), pick it up again to check that you are still on the right course. It is not that you have to be going in the same direction as I am, but by re-acquainting yourself with where you began, you will be better able to judge both how much progress you have made and how far this progress is worthwhile.

Beyond this, I do not believe I can help you, nor would it be beneficial if I could. If these skills are valuable, it is partly because they can be continued without a teacher. To provide a reading list would be irrelevant and perhaps boastful. I will give just one example to illustrate the sort of direction to take if you ever get lost.

Izaak Walton ends his book *The Compleat Angler* with a quotation from 1 Thessalonians 4.11: 'Study to be quiet.' That this is more than just an apt quotation can be guessed from the words with which he ends the epitaph to his wife Anne: 'Study to be like her.' Living and writing in the violent, dangerous and turbulent years of the English Civil War and the Commonwealth, the word 'study' has a particular strength of commitment.

What did he mean by it? Read the book; it is a treatise on the art of fishing, yet also one of the great spiritual classics. It is encouraging to note that Walton had a special love of poetry but was never very good at it; instead his persistent, unsuccessful efforts bore fruit in the quality of his prose, a quality that has made this the most often reprinted work in the English language, after the Bible and the Book of Common Prayer.

If in doubt, read the classics, not worrying about the subject so much as the quality, and knowing that wisdom grows as much in the manner of the reading as in the manner of the writing. For this reason, there is no reading list; it is the reading that matters, and this largely depends on the reader; indeed, there need not be any reading at all; angling itself might be the next step.

If sharing the vision of God brings us before life, the universe and everything, love, pain and death, then the limits of this book should be obvious. These modest, formal exercises are a beginning of wisdom. The fact that though simple to describe, they are so demanding to follow, and must be continued for so long a period of time, is evidence that they are only a small part of a greater whole.

These exercises have value precisely because they depend on so much else. This is the wonderful charm of wisdom, that we must always share our gift with others, and must rely upon them to do likewise. To receive a truth by revelation can be an intensely personal experience, but in wisdom such individualism would be ridiculous. If its knowledge is subjective, it must also be objective, public and open to anyone. This alone is reason to love it, that the more we receive the more we hold in common.